ST. BERNARD'S SERMONS

ON THE

NATIVITY

Nihil obstat:

FR. STANISLAUS HICKEY, O.C.R.,
Censor.

die 28ª Martii, 1921.

Imprimatur:

✠ FR. AUGUSTINUS MARRE,
Ep. t. Constant.
Abbas Generalis O.C.R

die 2ª Aprilis, 1921.

Nihil obstat:

GULIELMUS CANONICUS BYRNE, S.T.L.,
Censor deputatus.

Imprimi potest:

✠ BERNARDUS,
Episcopus Waterfordiensis
et Lismorensis.

WATERFORDIAE, die 1ª Aprilis, 1921.

Printed by

MASLANDS LTD, TIVERTON

and published October 1985 by

AUGUSTINE PUBLISHING CO, CHULMLEIGH, DEVON,
EX18 7HL

ST. BERNARD'S SERMONS

ON THE

NATIVITY

TRANSLATED FROM THE ORIGINAL LATIN

BY

A PRIEST OF MOUNT MELLERAY

DEVON, MCMLXXXV

Isaias. ix.

light shall shine upon us this day : for our Lord is born to us; and he shall be called Wonderful, God, the prince of peace, the father of the world to come; of whose reign there shall be no end. *Ps.* The Lord hath reigned, he is clothed with beauty: the Lord is clothed with strength, and hath girded himself. ℣. Glory.

Introit for the Mass at Day-break on Christmas Day.

CONTENTS

SERMONS FOR ADVENT

SERMONS FOR CHRISTMAS EVE

CONTENTS

ST. BERNARD'S SERMONS

FOR THE SEASONS AND THE PRINCIPAL FESTIVALS

FIRST SERMON FOR ADVENT

ON THE COMING OF CHRIST AND THE CIRCUMSTANCES WHICH ATTENDED IT

" Behold I come."—Ps. xxxix. 8.

TO-DAY, my brethren, we celebrate the beginning of the season of advent. The name of this, as of all our other solemnities, is familiar enough and well known to the entire world. But perhaps the meaning of the name is not so generally understood. For the unhappy children of Adam, taken up as they are with the pursuit of things transitory and perishable, pay but little attention to what is salutary and true. "To what shall we liken" the men of this generation, "or to what shall we compare" them, those, I mean, who, as we see, cannot be drawn or weaned away from earthly and material consolations? They resemble persons who have suffered shipwreck and are now battling for their lives in the water. You know with what desperate tenacity such people cling to everything they chance to lay hold of and refuse, on any account, to let it go, whatever it happens to be, even though it be something which cannot in the least help them to save themselves, for example, the roots of a plant, or some other such frail object. And should some of the witnesses of their peril venture forth to assist them, the drowning men are wont to clasp them so closely that they—the would-be rescuers—are rendered powerless to save either themselves or those whom they have come to succour. So do sinners perish in " this great sea which stretcheth wide its arms," so perish miserable mortals, because whilst they devote themselves to the pursuit of the unstable goods of nature and fortune, they lose the more solid goods of grace, by firmly cling-ing to which they would have escaped the danger and saved their souls. For it is not of vanity but of truth that the Saviour has promised, " You shall know it and it shall make you free." Do you, therefore, my breth-ren, to whom, as to His little ones, God reveals what is hidden from the wise and prudent, do you, I say, ponder well, in assiduous meditation, those things which are truly salutary, and diligently reflect on the meaning of this advent, asking yourselves, Who is He that comes ? whence does He come ? to what place does He come ? for what purpose does He come ? at what time does He come ? by what road does He come ? Such curi-osity is evidently as commendable as it is wholesome. For the universal Church would not observe this season of advent with so much devotion unless she knew that some great and holy mystery lies hidden therein.

In the first place, therefore, let us also, like the Apostle, be overwhelmed with awe and admiration whilst we consider the infinite greatness of Him Whose coming we celebrate. For, according to the testimony of the Angel Gabriel, He is the Son of the Most High, and consequently is Himself also Most High. It would be blasphemy to suppose the Son of God unworthy of His Father. So we must confess that the Father and the Son are equally exalted and one and the same in Majesty. Who does not know that the sons of princes are themselves princes and that the sons of kings are kings? Yet the question may be asked—why is it that of the Three Divine Persons Whom we believe, Whom we confess, Whom we adore in the Sovereign Trinity, it is not the Father, nor the Holy Ghost, but the Son Who comes to us? To me it appears manifest that there must be some special reason for this. But " who hath known the mind of the Lord? Or who hath been His counsellor? " So much at least is certain, that the coming of the Second Person was not decreed without a solemn counsel of the Most Blessed Trinity. And perhaps if we consider the cause of our banishment, we shall be able to understand in some degree how fitting it was that the Son especially should be our Deliverer. Lucifer, he who " arose in the morning," was instantly hurled down from the height of heaven, because he attempted as a usurper to make himself like to the Most High and as a robber would pretend to an equality with God, which is the exclusive pre-rogative of the Son. For the Father exercised His zeal in defence of the Son's glory, and by His action seemed to express what He afterwards spoke through His Prophet, " Revenge to Me, I will repay." Imme-diately that happened whereof Christ speaks when He says, " I saw Satan, as lightning, falling from heaven." What motive, then, hast thou for pride, thou who art but dust and ashes? If God has not spared the proud princes of heaven, how much less will He spare pride in thee, a mass of rottenness and worms ? Lucifer performed no criminal action, he was guilty of no evil deed, his only sin was a proud thought, and " in a moment, in the twinkling of an eye," he was precipitated down in irreparable ruin, because, as the Evangelist says, " He stood not in the truth."

Therefore, dearest brethren, keep far away from pride. Shun it, I beg of you, with all possible diligence, " for pride is the beginning of all sin," that pride which so swiftly overcast with a cloud of eternal darkness the glory of Lucifer, whose·brightness had eclipsed the very stars of heaven, that pride which changed into demons not only an angel but the very first and highest of the angels. Hence, he at once grew envious of man, and the iniquity which he had conceived in himself he brought forth in our first parents, persuading them that, by tasting the forbidden fruit, they should become like God, knowing good and evil. O miserable one, what art thou promising them ? What art thou holding out to their hope ? It is not to thee but to the Son of the Most High that belongs the key of knowledge. Yea, He is Himself " the Key of David That openeth and no man shutteth." " In Him are hid all the treasures of wisdom and knowledge." And wilt thou have the power and the impious daring to steal those treasures therefrom, in order that thou mayest deliver them to man ? You thus perceive, my brethren, how Lucifer, according to the words of Christ, "'is a liar and the father thereof." For he became a liar when he said, " I will be like the Most High," and the father of lies when he infused into man also the poisoned seed of his falsity, with the words, " You shall be as gods." But thou too, O man, "if thou didst see the thief, thou didst run with him."

You have heard, my brethren, what was read to us from the Prophet Isaias in the office of vigils last night : " Thy princes are faithless, the companions of thieves," or, as it is read in another version :* " Thy princes are disobedient, the companions of thieves." In truth, Adam and Eve, who are our princes (*principes*), as being the first parents of our race, became ' disobedient and the companions of thieves " when, at the suggestion of the serpent, or rather of the devil in the serpent, they attempted to usurp the prerogative of the Son of God. Nor did the Father regard with indifference the dishonour done to His Son, " for the Father loveth the Son," as the Evangelist assures us. Rather He took summary vengeance on the transgressors, and instantly His hand commenced to weigh heavy upon us all. For we have all sinned in Adam, and in him likewise we have all received the sentence of condemnation. Now what will the Son do, seeing the Father full of zeal for His glory and sparing no creature to avenge the injury done it ? " Behold," He seems to say, " the Father, on My account, has lost many of His intelligent creatures. The first of the angels ambitioned My Majesty, and he found many to support his pretensions. But the zeal of My Father wreaked instant and terrible vengeance upon him, smiting both him and his followers with an incurable plague, a most fearful chastisement. Man also endeavoured to usurp the knowledge which equally belongs to Me, and him, likewise, My Father punished without mercy, neither hath His eye spared

---

* He means the Septuagint Version which has : " οἱ ἄρκοντές σου ἀπειθοῦσι, κοινωνοὶ κλεπτῶν."—(Translator.)

him. ' Doth God take care for oxen ? ' Only two
orders of noble creatures has He made, endowed with
the gift of understanding and with the capacity for
eternal happiness, the angelic, namely, and the human.
And lo ! because of Me He has suffered the loss of many
angels and of all men. Therefore that they ' may know
that I love the Father,' He shall have restored to Him
through Me those whom through Me—in some sense at
least—He seems to have lost. ' Take me up,' then, ye
despairing ones, ' and cast Me into the sea, for I know
that for My sake this great tempest is upon you.'* All
are envious of Me. Therefore, ' behold I come,' and I
will show Myself to them in such a character that for
all who may wish to envy Me, and for all who may
strive to imitate Me, this envy and this emulation shall
turn to their advantage. I know, nevertheless, that
the apostate angels ' have passed into an affection of
the heart ' in ' malice and wickedness,' and that their
sin has not the excuse of ignorance or infirmity. Consequently, as they refuse to repent, it is necessary that
they perish. For the Father's affection as well as
' the honour of the King loveth judgment.' "†

It was, indeed, for this reason that God in the beginning created men, in order, namely, to fill up the places
left vacant by the fall of the angels and to repair the
ruins of the heavenly Jerusalem.‡ For He knew that

* Allusion to Jonas i. 12.—(Translator.)

† This is one of the three reasons assigned by St. Thomas
to show how congruous it was that the Second Person should
become incarnate rather than the First or Third (*Sum. Theol.*,
III. q. iii. a. 8). For the other " congruities " or " conveni-
ences " which theologians have discerned in the Incarnation
of the Word, see Faber's *Bethlehem*, pp. 21-27.—(Translator.)

‡ This opinion seems to have been very common amongst
the Fathers, and was even supposed to be implied in certain
passages of Scripture. Thus the celebrated Peter Lombard,
the " Master of the Sentences," says of it : " De homine quoque

for these rebellious spirits there was no possibility of
a return to grace, being aware " of the pride of Moab,
that he is exceeding proud," and that his pride does
not admit the remedy of repentance, nor, consequently, the remedy of pardon.   But when man also
fell, He, the Creator, produced no new order of creatures
to make good the loss.   Thus He intimated that the
human race was to be redeemed, because, as it had
been seduced by a malice not its own, it could also be
saved by a charity not its own.   According to Thy
merciful design, therefore, " be pleased, O Lord, to
deliver me, for I am weak."   Like Joseph " I was
stolen away out of my native land, and here without
any fault was cast into the dungeon."   I do not pretend indeed to be absolutely innocent, I only claim a
relative innocence : that my guilt is as nothing compared to the guilt of him who seduced me.   He led me,
O Lord, to assent to a lie.   Let truth come, therefore,
in order that his falsity may be exposed.   So shall I
know the truth and the truth shall make me free,
if yet I renounce completely the lie when unmasked
and cleave to the truth when ascertained.   Were I to
act otherwise, I should no longer be yielding to a human
temptation, nor committing a human sin, but making

in Scriptura interdum reperitur quod factus sit propter repara-
tionem angelicae ruinae."   But, he adds, " quod non ita est
intelligendum quasi non fuisset homo factus si non pecasset
angelus, sed quia inter alias causas, scilicet, praecipuas, haec
etiam nonnulla causa extitit."   It is at the present time less
generally held, because (amongst other reasons) of its apparent
incompatibility with the doctrine maintained by Scotus and
Suarez against St. Thomas, and now widely accepted, namely,
that amongst the divine operations *ad extra* the Incarnation
was decreed first and chiefly, as being the end and motive
of all the others, so that even though the angels and man had
remained faithful, Christ would still have taken flesh.   Cf.
Hurter, *Theol. dogm.*, vol. ii. 347-50.—(Translator.)

myself guilty of diabolical obstinacy. For to continue voluntarily in evil is the sin of the devil ; and they who choose to imitate his perseverance in sin deserve to be his associates in everlasting perdition.

You have now heard, my brethren, Who it is that comes. Consider next whence He comes and whither : He comes from the Heart of God the Father into the womb of a Virgin Mother : He comes from the highest heavens to the lowest parts of the earth. What then ? Are not we also under the necessity of living on the earth ? Aye, and it will be a painful exile for us unless He consents to keep us company. For where can it be well with us without Him ? Or with Him where can it be ill with us ?* " What have I in heaven ? And besides Thee what do I desire upon earth ? For Thee my flesh and my heart hath fainted away : Thou art the God of my heart and the God That is my portion for ever." " For though I should walk in the midst of the shadow of death, I will fear no evils, (provided) Thou art with Me." Now, as I perceive, He descends to the earth, and even into hell, not however as a captive, but as one Who is " free among the dead." For " He is the Light (That) shineth in darkness, and the darkness did not comprehend It." Therefore, according to the words of David, His Soul was not left in hell, nor did His Body see corruption in the heart of the earth. For Christ " Who descended is the Same also That ascended above all the heavens, that He might fill all things." Of Him it is written that " He went about doing good, and healing all that were oppressed by the devil," and also that, " He hath

* " To be without Jesus is a grievous hell, and to be with Jesus is a sweet paradise. If Jesus be with thee, no enemy can hurt thee."—*Imitation of Christ*, Bk. II. ch. viii.

rejoiced as a giant to run His way : His going out is from the end of heaven, and His circuit even to the end thereof." Good reason, then, has the Apostle to cry out to us, saying, " Seek the things that are above, where Christ is sitting at the Right Hand of God." But he would have laboured in vain to lift our hearts to heaven, unless he could show us the Author of our salvation enthroned there. However, let us now pass on to consider the remaining points. For although the matter is extremely rich and abundant, the shortness of the time at our disposal will not allow us to deal with it at adequate length. To sum up the results of our enquiries so far : the question as to Who is He That comes, has brought before us a Majesty infinitely sublime and ineffable ; and, when we lifted up our eyes to discover whence He comes, we beheld a road of immeasurable length, according to the testimony of Isaias, who, filled with the prophetic spirit, exclaimed, " Behold the name of the Lord cometh from afar " ; finally, on considering whither He comes, we have been led to realise that most admirable but utterly incom-prehensible loving-kindness whereby the infinite Majesty of God has honoured us by coming down into the gloomy abode of our prison.

Now who can doubt that there must be interests of paramount importance at stake when the Divine Majesty deigned to descend from an eminence so sublime to a place so unworthy ? The object must surely be some-thing great, since the mercy is so great, and the kindness so great, and so great too the charity. What, then, shall we say is the purpose for which the Son of the Most High has come down amongst us ? For this is the question which, in the order I have proposed to follow, comes next for discussion. Here, however, we shall not have far to seek for an answer, since the Lord Himself, by His words and actions, has clearly proclaimed the cause of His coming. He descended in haste from the heavenly hills to seek the one sheep of His hundred which had strayed from the fold : He came down for our sakes, in order that, more manifestly than before, " the mercies of the Lord might give praise to Him and His wonderful works to the children of men." Oh, how marvellous a condescension in God to come down from heaven in quest of man ! And how great an honour to man so to be sought by God ! Surely " though we should have a mind to glory " in such an honour " we shall not be foolish." Not that man seems to be anything as of himself, but because He Who made him has made so much of him. For all the riches and all the glory of the world, and whatever else it possesses which the human heart may desire, all this is little, yea, it is nothing at all in comparison with the honour of being sought after by God. O Lord, " what is a man that Thou shouldst magnify him ? Or why dost Thou set Thy Heart upon him ? "

Nevertheless, I should like to know the reason why He has come to us, and why did not we rather go to Him. For it is we who have need of Him, not He of us.* Thus, amongst men, it is not the custom of the rich to visit the poor, even when they wish to give them assistance. Such in truth is the case, my brethren : it were more fitting that we should go to Him than that He should come to us. But there were two obstacles which prevented our access. For, in the

* " Thou hast need of Me, not I of thee."—*Imitation of Christ*, Bk. IV. ch. xii.

first place, our eyes were weak and dim, whereas He "inhabiteth light inaccessible " ; and, secondly, we were as the paralytic lying helpless in his bed, and could not by any means attain to the loftiness of the Divine Majesty. Therefore, our most benign Saviour, the tender Physician of our souls, descended from His throne on high and tempered His glory's splendour to the weakness of our vision. For He, " the Brightness of eternal Light," enclosed Himself in the lantern, so to speak, of that glorious, that most pure and spotless Flesh Which He took from a virgin mother, and which is manifestly signified by that most light and luminous cloud upon which, according to the prediction of Isaias, the Lord was to ascend, in order that He might come down into Egypt.*

I now proceed to the consideration of the time at which the Saviour made His advent. He came (as I am sure you do not need to be told) not at the beginning of the world's history, nor in the middle, but towards the end. This was not without good reason : it was a wise disposition of infinite Wisdom, Who, knowing how prone to ingratitude are the children of Adam, decreed to defer sending them succour until the time of their greatest necessity. It was then, indeed, " towards evening and the day (was) now far spent," since the Sun of Justice had almost disappeared from the gaze of mortals, and very little of His light or heat any longer reached the earth. I mean to say, the light of the knowledge of God had become exceedingly dim, and, whilst iniquity abounded, charity had lost its fervour and had grown cold. The angels had ceased to show themselves, and the prophets preached no longer. It

* Isaias xix. I.

seemed as if they had given up in despair, frustrated in their efforts by the incredible hardness and obstinacy of men. It was then that the Son of God spoke to the Father, saying, " Behold I come." Thus, thus, O Lord, " while all things were in quiet silence, and night was in the midst of her course, Thy almighty Word leapt down from heaven from Thy royal throne." The Apostle Paul is alluding to the same circumstance of the time when he says, " But when the fulness of time was come, God sent His Son." For the fulness and plenty of the good things that belong to time had produced spiritual indigence, and even forgetfulness, as regards the goods of eternity. Opportunely, therefore, the eternal appeared to compete with the temporal at the moment when the latter had attained its fullest development.* For, to say nothing of other things, so great was the peace then prevailing amongst men, that at the bidding of a single ruler the whole world was enrolled.

You now understand, my brethren, Who it is That comes ; you know whence He comes and whither ; and you know also the time and the cause of His coming. Only one point more remains to be examined, namely, by what road does He come ? We must labour with all diligence to ascertain this, in order that (as is proper) we may be able to go forth to meet Him in the way. Now, just as He came once for all visibly and in the flesh to " work our salvation in the midst of earth," so He comes daily, in spirit and invisibly, to save indi-

---

* That is to say, the Son of God, in order to enhance the glory of His triumph over the world in the competition for human hearts, delayed to manifest Himself until temporal prosperity had attained its highest perfection. Cf. St. Thomas, *Sum. Theol.*, III. q. i. a. 4.—(Translator.)

vidual souls. Hence it is written, " A Spirit before our face is Christ the Lord." And to give us to understand that this spiritual advent is secret, the Prophet continues, " Under Thy shadow we shall live among the gentiles." It is therefore becoming, if the sick man cannot go forth any distance to meet so august a Physician, that he should at least show Him honour on His arrival by making an effort to raise his head and to sit up in his couch. There is no necessity for thee, O man, to cross the seas, or to penetrate the clouds, or to pass over the mountains. Thou art not invited to undertake any great journey. Even within thine own soul rise to meet thy God. For it is written : " The Word is nigh thee, even in thy mouth and in thy heart." Rise to welcome Him by compunction of the heart and by confession of the mouth, so that thou mayest issue forth in His honour, at least from the sink of thy miserable conscience ; for it would be a grievous crime to introduce hither the Author of all purity. So much concerning this spiritual advent of the Word, whereby He condescends to illumine with His invisible presence the soul of every one of us.

But it is also a delight for me to consider the road by which He came to us visibly, because " His ways are beautiful ways and all His paths are peaceful." " Behold," exclaims the Spouse in the Canticle, " behold He cometh leaping upon the mountains, skipping over the hills." Thou now seest Him coming to thee, O beautiful Bride of the Word ; but before thou couldst not discover Him, whilst He was reclining in repose. For thou didst say to Him, " Shew me, O Thou Whom my soul loveth, where Thou feedest, where Thou liest in the mid-day." He reclines at ease where for endless ages He pastures His flock of celestial spirits, feeding them with the vision of His own eternity and immutability. But, O beautiful one, be not ignorant of thyself and thy capacity. That vision which thou desirest " is become wonderful to thee, it is high and thou canst not reach to it." But behold, He has come forth from His holy place. He Who reclining feeds the angels, " He hath taken us and He will heal us." And He Who before could not be seen whilst reclining and feeding the angels, shall now be made manifest, visibly coming and visibly fed. " Behold He cometh, leaping upon the mountains, skipping over the hills." By these mountains and hills understand the prophets and apostles. And in what sense He came leaping and skipping you shall find explained in the " Book of generation," " Abraham begot Isaac, and Isaac begot Jacob," etc. From these mountains, as you shall see, grew out the root of Jesse, from which, according to the prediction of the Prophet Isaias, a rod came forth, and from the rod a flower, whereon the sevenfold Spirit hath rested. The same Prophet has declared this more explicitly in another place, where he says, " Behold a virgin shall conceive and bear a Son, and His name shall be called Emmanuel, which, being interpreted, is God with us." For Him Whom before he called a Flower, he here calls Emmanuel, and the rod from which he said the Flower was to spring, he now explains to signify a virgin. However, the consideration of this most profound mystery must be postponed to another day ; for it is a subject that deserves a special sermon to itself, and besides, to-day's discourse has already been sufficiently prolonged.

SECOND SERMON FOR ADVENT

On the Words of the Prophet Isaias to King Achaz

" Ask thee a sign of the Lord thy God, either unto the depth of hell, or unto the height above. And Achaz said : I will not ask, and I will not tempt the Lord. And he said : Hear ye, therefore, O house of David : Is it a small thing for you to be grievous to men that you are grievous to my God also ? Therefore the Lord Himself shall give you a sign. Behold a virgin shall conceive and bear a Son, and His name shall be called Emmanuel. He shall eat butter and honey, that He may know to refuse evil and to choose the good."—Is. vii. 11-16.

My brethren, we have heard the Prophet urging King Achaz to " ask a sign of the Lord either unto the depth of hell or unto the height above." We have also heard the King's answer, vested indeed in the semblance of piety, but containing nothing of the virtue. For this reason he deserved to be rejected by Him Who seeth the heart, and to Whom " the thought of man confesseth." " I will not ask," he said, " and I will not tempt the Lord." The royal state and dignity had puffed him up with pride, and, being full of craft, he knew how to speak the words of human wisdom. Therefore, Isaias received from the Lord the command, " Go and say to that fox : Ask thee a sign of the Lord thy God unto the depth of hell,"—by which is meant that although this crafty fox has his den of cunning deep down, yet even should he descend into hell, there is One Who " will catch the wise in their own craftiness." Again He commanded the Prophet, " Go and say to this bird : Ask thee a sign of the

15

Lord unto the height above." That is, this ambitious
bird has built himself a nest on high ; yet, even though
he should ascend into heaven, he shall there find One
Who " resisteth the proud," and Who, by His own
might, tramples on the necks of the arrogant and high-
minded. King Achaz, however, refuses to ask a sign
either of God's exalted power, or of the incomprehensible
profundity of His wisdom ; and hence the Lord Himself promises to the house of David a sign of goodness
and charity, so that those whom neither the exhibitions
of power nor of wisdom could terrify may be attracted
at least by the manifestation of love. Yet the words,
" unto the depth of hell," may be taken, not unreasonably, to refer to this very charity of God, " greater
than which no man hath," and which caused Him to
die and to descend into hell for those whom He loved.
According to this interpretation, Achaz is bidden, either
to tremble at the Majesty of Him Who reigns on high,
or else to respond to the charity of Him Who out of
love descends into hell. Therefore, whosoever does not
think of this Majesty with fear, and reflect on this
charity with a return of love, is not only " grievous to
men " but is " grievous to God also." " Because of
this," the Prophet replies, " the Lord Himself shall
give you a sign (in which both majesty and love shall
be clearly revealed). Behold a virgin shall conceive and
bear a Son, and His name shall be called Emmanuel,
which being interpreted is, God with us." O Adam,
flee not away from Him, because now He is " God
with us." Tremble not, O man, and quake not so with
terror on hearing the name of God, for now it is " God
with us." God is with us in the likeness of the flesh.
He is with us by identity of nature. For our sakes He

has come, and He has come as one of ourselves, " passible like unto us."

" He shall eat butter and honey," that is to say, He shall be a Little One, and shall be nourished with such food as is suitable for infants. " That He may know to refuse the evil and to choose the good." Here also, my brethren, just as in the case of the forbidden fruit, as in the case of the tree of transgression, we have good and evil presented for choice. But the second Adam makes a far wiser election than the first ; for He chooses the good, and rejects the evil : not like him who " loved cursing and it came upon him, and he would not have a blessing and it was far from him." The words just preceding, " He shall eat butter and honey," indicate, as you may notice, the choice made by this Little One. Only let Him assist me now with His grace, so that I may be able to express worthily and intelligently the ideas which by Him have been suggested to my mind. There are two kinds of food made from the milk of the sheep, namely, butter and cheese. Butter is moist and oily, cheese is dry and hard. Well, therefore, does our Little One know how to choose, since He eats the butter and refuses the cheese. That hundredth sheep which, as the Gospel tells us, wandered from the fold, and in whose name the Psalmist sings, " I have gone astray like a sheep that is lost," that sheep, my brethren, represents the human race which the loving-kind Shepherd comes in quest of, leaving His other ninety-nine sheep on the mountains. Now in this stray sheep there are two things to be considered : its nature, which, like butter, is sweet and good, and precious ; and the corruption wrought in it by sin, of which cheese is a symbol. See therefore what an admirable choice our Little One has made, assuming to Himself our nature, but without its sinful corruption. Of sinners you may remember to have read in the psalm, " Their heart is curdled like milk," because in them the " leaven of malice " and the curd of iniquity have corrupted the pure milk of their nature.

In the bee also there are two opposing properties. The sweetness of its honey is matched by the bitterness of its sting. But there is a Bee That " feedeth among the lilies," That lives in the flower-bedecked land of the angels. And because He loves the flowers, He flew down to the village of Nazareth, the very name of which signifies a flower ; and coming to a sweet smelling blossom of perpetual virginity, thereon He lighted, thereon He remained. The honey and the sting of this Bee will not be forgotten by him who, with the Psalmist, sings " to the Lord mercy and judgment." Nevertheless, when He descended to us, He brought but the honey, leaving the sting behind. That is to say, the Word came to us bringing mercy without judgment. Hence, on one occasion, when the disciples urged Him to give command that a certain city, which had refused to admit Him, should be consumed by fire from heaven, He replied that " the Son of man came not to destroy souls, but to save." This Bee of ours was then without any sting. He had in a manner laid it aside whilst He exercised mercy without judgment in the case of those who treated Him with so much cruelty and indignity. But, my brethren, " trust not in iniquity," sin not in hope. The time will come when our Bee shall resume His sting, aye, and with exceeding ferocity shall plunge it into the sinner's very vitals ; " for neither doth the Father judge any man, but hath given all judgment to the Son." Now, however, our Little One eateth butter and honey by uniting in Himself the divine mercy with the good of human nature, in such a way that He is made a true Man without any participation in human sin, and a God of mercy, dissembling judgment.

These observations, as I hope, have enabled you to understand what that rod is which was to " come forth out of the root of Jesse," and what the Flower Which was to " rise up out of his root," on Which, it was predicted, the Spirit of the Lord should rest. For the rod signifies Mary, the Virgin Mother of God, and the Flower represents her Son. Truly a Flower is the Virgin's Child, " a Flower, white and ruddy, chosen out of thousands," a Flower on Which " the angels desire to look," a Flower Whose fragrance gives life to the dead, and, as He calls Himself, " the Flower of the field," not of the garden. For the field produces its flowers without the co-operation of man, unsown by human hand, unploughed, unprepared by human labour. Thus, my brethren, thus beyond a doubt, flourished the holy Virgin's womb ; thus inviolate, thus intact and un-spotted,* as a field of unfading greenness, it produced its divine Flower, a Flower Whose beauty shall never see corruption, the splendour of Whose glory shall never grow dim. O glorious Virgin ! O Rod sublime " from the root of Jesse " ! To what a dizzy height dost thou lift thy sacred crest ! Even to Him Who sitteth on the throne, even to the Lord of Majesty ! Yet this should not astonish us, seeing that thou hast

---

* " Sic inviolata, integra, et casta Mariae viscera." Compare this with the opening words of the beautiful anthem so often sung at Benediction in Cistercian churches : " Inviolata, integra, et casta es, Maria."—(Translator.)

struck so deep the roots of thy humility. O truly
celestial plant, singularly holy, precious above all!
Verily thou art the tree of life, which alone has been
reputed worthy to bear the fruit of salvation. Thy
craft has been exposed, O malignant serpent, thy
deceit has been discovered. Two charges thou didst
bring against thy Creator; thou didst slanderously
accuse Him of falsehood and envy. With regard to
both thou art now thyself convicted of lying. For
they to whom thou didst say, " No, you shall not die
the death," did die, as a matter of fact, shortly after,
whilst " the truth of the Lord remaineth for ever."
And, as touching the second charge, tell me now, if
thou canst, what tree, or what fruit of any tree, could
God out of envy have forbidden man, to whom He has
not denied even this chosen tree " from the root of
Jesse," or the noble Fruit Which crowns it ? " He That
spared not even His own Son, but delivered Him up for
us all, how hath He not also with Him given us all
things ? "

You have already perceived, I suppose, that the
Virgin herself is the royal road by which the Saviour
came to us, issuing forth from her womb " as a Bridegroom from the bride-chamber." Therefore, my dearest
brethren, walking faithfully in this way (concerning
which I made some remarks in the preceding sermon
also, if you remember), let us endeavour by it to ascend
to Jesus, Who by the same has descended to us ; let us
strive, I say, to go by Mary to share His grace Who
by Mary came to share our misery. Through thee, O
most blessed One, Finder of grace, Mother of life, Mother
of salvation, through thee let us have access to thy
Son, so that through thee He may receive us Who was

given us through thee.   Let thy integrity excuse before
Him the foulness of our corruption ; let thy humility,
so pleasing to God, make amends and obtain pardon
for our pride ; let thy abounding charity cover the
multitude of our sins ; let thy glorious fecundity supply
in our behalf for a fecundity of merit.   O thou who
art our Lady, our Mediatrix, and our Advocate, reconcile us to thy Son, commend us to thy Son, present
us to thy Son.   Grant, O most blessed One, by the
grace thou has found, by the prerogative thou hast
merited, by the mercy thou hast obtained, that He
Who vouchsafed to make Himself, by thy consent and
co-operation, a partaker of our poverty and infirmity,
may make us by thy intercession partakers of His own
glory and happiness, Jesus Christ, thy Son and our
Lord, Who is over all things, God blessed for ever.
Amen.

THIRD SERMON FOR ADVENT

On the Three Advents of the Lord, and the Seven Pillars which we ought to erect within us

" Wisdom hath built herself a house, she hath hewn her out seven pillars."—Prov. ix. 1.

In this advent of Christ, my brethren, which we are now celebrating, I cannot think of the Person Who has come, without feeling overpowered in mind by the excellence of His Majesty ; and when I consider who they are to whom He has come, I tremble with awe at the greatness of His condescension. The angels certainly must contemplate with astonishment so unheard of a wonder, beholding now beneath them Him Whom they have always worshipped and shall ever worship as their Overlord, thus manifestly " ascending and descending to the Son of man." Again, when I reflect on the object of His coming, I embrace as well as I can the immeasurable extent of His charity. And if, finally, I meditate on the manner in which He has come, I realise and acknowledge the dignity to which our human nature has been raised. For He Who has come is the Creator and Lord of the universe, He has come to men, He has come for the sake of men, He has come a man. But some one may here object and say : " How can He be said to have come Who has always been everywhere ? " I answer in the words of the Evangelist, " He was in the world, and the world was made by Him, and the world knew Him not."

Therefore, when I speak of His coming, I do not mean that He began to be present where previously He was absent, but only that He made Himself manifest where before He had been concealed. Hence, in order to become visible to us, He even assumed our human nature, He Who in His Divinity " dwelleth in light inaccessible." Neither, assuredly, was it anything unbecoming the Creator's Majesty to appear in the form of that likeness of Himself which He had fashioned in the beginning, nor was it unworthy of God to be represented in an image to such as could not see Him in His own Divine Essence, so that He Who of old made man to His own image and likeness, might, at least as a man, become known to men.

Therefore, my brethren, once a year the universal Church makes a solemn commemoration of the advent of such Majesty, of such condescension, of such charity, yea, of such a glorification of the human race. Once a year—would to God it were once and for ever ! That would be far better. For surely men must be strangely infatuated when they have the desire or the daring to occupy themselves with any other interest after the advent of so great a King, instead of forgetting everything else in His presence and devoting themselves exclusively to His service and worship. But not of all can be understood the words of the Psalmist, " They shall eructate the memory of the abundance of Thy sweetness," for even to taste of this sweetness is not granted to all. And surely no one eructates what he has not tasted or what he has merely tasted. Eructation proceeds only from fulness and satiety. Therefore, men of worldly mind and worldly conduct, even though they celebrate the memory of this manifestation of divine sweetness, do not eructate that memory, but observe these holy days simply from custom, without fervour, without devotion, or any feeling of tenderness. And what is still worse, they even make this commemoration of God's infinite condescension an occasion for indulging the desires of the natural man. Hence you may see them during this time sparing no pains to procure splendid garments and costly viands, as if, forsooth, Christ looks for these and such-like things on the day of His nativity, and is there more worthily received where these are more scrupulously offered. But attend to what He has said Himself, " With him that had a proud eye and an insatiable heart, I would not eat." " Why," He seems to ask, " art thou so solicitous to provide thyself with a rich dress against My birthday ? So far from being pleased with such pride, I hold it in abhorrence. Wherefore all this anxiety to lay up such abundant supplies of food for Christmas-tide ? The pleasures of the palate are not acceptable to Me, but rather offensive. Verily, thou must be of an ' insatiable heart,' making such elaborate preparations and for so long a time. The body surely does not require so many things, and would be contented with that which is plain and easily procured. Therefore, in thus celebrating My advent, thou honourest me with thy lips, but thy heart is far from Me. I am not the object of thy worship, for thy god is thy stomach and thy glory is in thy shame. Oh, how unhappy art thou in thus paying homage to bodily pleasure and the vanity of worldly glory ! ' But happy is that people whose God is the Lord.' "

My brethren, " Be not emulous of evildoers, nor envy them that work iniquity." Consider rather their last

end, pity them from your hearts, and pray for all who
" are overtaken in sin." It is only from ignorance of
God that these miserable men have adopted such a
manner of celebrating Christmas. For did they know
the truth, they certainly would never provoke against
them by their incredible folly the anger of the Lord
of glory. But as for ourselves, my dearly beloved, we
have not the excuse of ignorance. To every one who
is here present I say, thou surely dost know Him. And
if thou wert to answer that thou knowest Him not,
thou shouldst be like to worldlings, a liar. For if thou
hast no knowledge of Him, who then hath brought
thee to this place, or how hast thou come hither?
Didst thou not know Him, when wouldst thou have
been persuaded to break so freely the bonds of natural
love and friendship, to renounce the delights of the
flesh and the vanities of the world, " to cast thy care
upon the Lord," and to transfer all thy solicitude to
Him, from Whom, as thine own conscience bears
witness, thou hadst merited no favour but rather
severe chastisement? What, I ask, could have induced thee to behave thus, if thou wert ignorant that
" the Lord is good to them that hope in Him, to the
soul that seeketh Him," unless thou also hadst known
that " the Lord is sweet and mild and plenteous in
mercy"? But how couldst thou have known this, if
not because He not only came to thee, but even came
into thee?

There are three distinct comings of the Lord of
which I know, His coming *to* men, His coming *into* men,
and His coming *against* men. He comes to all men
indifferently, but comes not into all or against all. His
coming to men and His coming against men are too

well known to need elucidation. But concerning the second advent, which is spiritual and invisible, listen to what He says Himself, " If any man love Me, he will keep My word, and My Father will love him, and We will come to him and will make Our abode with him." Blessed is the man with whom Thou, Lord Jesus, makest Thy abode ! Blessed he in whom " Wisdom hath built herself a house, and hath hewn out her seven pillars " ! Blessed is the soul which has become the seat of Wisdom ! Shall I tell you whose this soul is ? She is the soul of the just man. This is manifest from the words of David, " Justice and judgment are the preparation of Thy throne." Is there any one amongst you, brethren, who desires to prepare a seat for Christ in his soul ? Behold here the kind of silk and embroidery with which He requires that the cushion shall be covered. Justice is a virtue which inclines us to give everyone his due. Now there are three classes of persons in relation to whom this virtue must be exercised, thy superiors, thy inferiors, and thy equals. Render therefore to those above thee, to those beneath thee, and to those on a level with thee, that which thou owest to each, and so shalt thou worthily celebrate the advent of Christ, adorning His seat for Him with justice. Render, I say, to thy superiors obedience and reverence, of which the first relates to thy exterior, whilst the second belongs to the heart. For it is not enough to show ourselves externally obedient to those in authority, unless we also entertain feelings of respect and veneration for them in the interior of our souls. And even should the life of any superior be so notoriously wicked as to admit of no excuse or dissimulation, nevertheless, for God's sake, Who is the Source of all power, we are bound to honour such a one, not on account of his personal merits, which are non-existent, but because of the divine ordination and the dignity of his office.

In like manner, the laws of fraternity and of human society give our brethren, amongst whom we live, a claim upon us for counsel and assistance. For we, on our side, desire that they should render us the same services, counsel to instruct our ignorance, assistance to support our weakness. But perchance there is some one here who is saying to himself in the silence of his heart, " What counsel can I give my brother, since I am not allowed to speak even one word to him without permission ? And how shall I assist him, who am not permitted to do anything whatever except under obedience ? " To this I answer, thou shalt never be in want of something to do so long as thou art not wanting in fraternal charity. In my judgment, there can be no better counsel than that which thou givest, when, by thy example thou dost strive to teach thy brother what is expedient for him to do and what to omit, urging him on to better things, and exhorting him " not in word nor in tongue, but in deed and in truth." And what better or more efficacious assistance can be given him than to pray for him with fervour, to reprove him frankly for his faults,* to place no obstacle in his path, but on the contrary, like an angel of peace, to be solicitous to " gather out of the kingdom of God all scandals," as far as is possible, and to remove from his way every occasion of stumbling ? When thou showest thyself such a counsellor and such

---

* That is, by accusations in chapter : for, as the Saint has just remarked, no private religious was permitted to speak to another.—(Translator.)

a helper to thy brother, then, in truth, thou art ren-
dering unto him that which thou owest, and he has
no cause to complain of thee.   But if, further, thou
art invested with authority over anyone, to him beyond
question thou owest a debt of greater solicitude. He
claims from thee watchfulness and correction : watchfulness, which shall enable him to avoid sin, correction
which shall allow no transgressions to remain unpun-
ished.   And even though none of thy brethren has been
committed to thy charge, there is nevertheless, one that
is subject to thee and that requires at thy hands the
same watchfulness and zeal.   I allude to thine own
body, which undoubtedly has been given thee in order
to be ruled by thy spirit.   Thou art therefore obliged
to watch over it so that " sin may not reign in it," and
that its members may not become " instruments of
iniquity." It has also a right to thy zealous correction,
so that, chastised and reduced to servitude, it may
"bring forth fruits worthy of penance." Yet far heavier
and far more perilous is the responsibility which weighs
upon him who has to render an account for many
souls.   " Unhappy man that I am," what shall I do
or whither shall I flee, if I am found to have negligently
guarded this immense treasure, this priceless deposit,
which Christ has judged more precious than His own
most precious Blood ?   Had I collected the Blood of
the Lord as It dripped and trickled from His Body on
the cross, and had I retained It in my possession, sealed
up in a vessel of glass, which I should be under the
necessity of carrying about with me constantly, oh,
how terrible would be my anxiety amidst so many
dangers ! And yet, my brethren, I have been made custo-
dian of something for which no imprudent Merchant,

yea, He Who is Wisdom Itself, did not hesitate to barter all that Blood. What is more, I am keeping " this treasure in earthen vessels," which seem to be exposed to perils greater and more numerous than vessels of glass. And further, to crown my solicitude and lest anything should be wanting to my fear, whilst I am obliged to watch over my own conscience and the consciences of my brethren, not one of these is sufficiently known to me. Each is to me an unfathomable abyss, a night of impenetrable darkness, and nevertheless I am charged with the custody of each, and the voice of the Lord is ever ringing in my ears, " Watchman, what of the night ? watchman, what of the night ? " It is not lawful for me to reply with Cain, " Am I my brother's keeper ? " No, I can only humble myself and confess with the Prophet that " unless the Lord keep the city, he watcheth in vain who keepeth it." I shall, however, be held excused if, as I have said, I am faithful in the discharge of my twofold function of vigilance and correction.* And if I am found to have satisfied the other four obligations also, by showing obedience and reverence to my superiors, and by giving counsel and help to my equals then, as regards

---

* " Let the Abbot always bear in mind that he will have to render an account both of his preaching and of the obedience of his disciples at the dreadful tribunal of God. He should likewise remember that the shepherd is held responsible for any want of improvement his Master may observe in the sheep ; and that he shall escape condemnation on the day of judgment only by showing that he had done his utmost to reform his unruly flock, and to apply the proper remedies for the cure of their diseases. Then indeed the shepherd, being acquitted at God's tribunal, can say with the Prophet ' I have not hid Thy justice within my heart ; I have declared Thy truth and Thy salvation, but they have despised me.' And finally eternal death shall be the portion of his disobedient flock."—Holy Rule of St. Benedict, ch. ii. (Mount Melleray Translation).

justice at any rate, Wisdom shall not find her seat
in my soul altogether unprepared.

And perhaps we have here six of the seven pillars
which Wisdom "hath hewn her out" in the house
which she hath "built herself." We must therefore
endeavour to find the seventh also, if haply she herself
will condescend to make it known to us. But as the
six which we have discovered belong to justice, why
should we not suppose the seventh to appertain to
judgment? For not justice alone, but "justice and
judgment are the preparation of Thy throne," O Lord.
Besides, if we render what we owe to our superiors,
to our equals, and to our inferiors, shall there be
nothing for God? It is doubtless true that we can
never discharge our debt to Him, because He has so
abundantly multiplied His mercies upon us, because we
have so often sinned against Him, because we are so
weak and worthless, and because He is so rich in
Himself and self-sufficing, "needing none of our goods."
Nevertheless hear what is said by holy David, to whom
He hath made manifest "the uncertain and hidden
things of His wisdom": "The honour of the King,"
sings the Royal Prophet, "loveth judgment." So far
as concerns Himself, there is nothing which He more
strictly requires from us. Only let us confess our
iniquities, and for the glory of His grace, He will
justify us freely. For He loves the soul which is constantly examining herself in His sight and judging
herself with sincerity. And it is only for our own
sakes He exacts this judgment from us, because if we
judge ourselves we shall not be judged. The wise man,
consequently, will be watchful and suspicious of all his
works, he will examine, scrutinise, and pass judgment

on everything ; and he who thus endeavours truly to know and who humbly confesses the value set by truth on himself and his works, shows that he honours truth. But I shall give you a more evident proof that judgment is required of us after justice : " When you have done all things that are commanded you," so speaks the Saviour, " say : we are unprofitable servants." As regards ourselves, therefore, we may rest assured that we are worthily preparing a seat within us for the Lord of Majesty, when we are striving to observe all the commandments of His justice, and are at the same time judging ourselves to be unprofitable servants.

FOURTH SERMON FOR ADVENT

ON TRUE AND FALSE VIRTUE AND THAT OUR VIRTUES MUST BE MODELLED ON THE VIRTUES OF CHRIST

" Length of days is in (His) right hand, and in (His) left hand riches and glory."—Prov. iii. 16.

It is fitting, my brethren, that we should celebrate this season of advent with all possible devotion, rejoicing in so great a consolation, marvelling at so great a condescension, inflamed with love by so great a manifestation of charity. But let us not think of that advent only whereby the Son of man has " come to seek and to save that which was lost," but also of that other by which He will come again and will take us to Himself. Would to God you kept these two advents constantly in your thoughts, revolving them in assiduous meditation, pondering in your hearts how much we have received by the first, how much we are promised at the second ! Would to God you were able thus to " sleep among the midst of lots " !* For these two comings of the Lord are the two arms of the Bridegroom, between which the Bride was sleeping when she said, " His Left Hand is under my head, and His

---

* " If you sleep among the midst of lots, you shall be as the wings of a dove, covered with silver, and the hinder parts of her back with the paleness of gold " (Ps. lxvii. 14). This is one of the most difficult verses in the whole psalter. According to most commentators, to " sleep among the midst of lots " signifies to rest in the truth of the Old and New Testaments, or to devote oneself alternately to the exercises of the active and contemplative life, or to die between the hope of heavenly happiness and the contempt of worldly enjoyments. Cf. Bellarmin's Commentary.—(Translator.)

Right shall embrace me " ; because, as we read elsewhere, " Length of days is in (His) Right Hand, and
in (His) Left Hand riches and glory." " In His Left
Hand riches and glory," so speaks the inspired author
of the Book of Proverbs. Attend to this, ye sons of
Adam, slaves to avarice and ambition. What concern
have you with earthly riches and temporal glory,
which are neither solid nor subject to your dominion ?
Silver and gold !   What are these but clay of the
earth, coloured white and yellow, which the error of
men alone makes, or rather reputes, of value ? I say
they are not subject to your dominion, for if they are,
why, then, not take them away with you? But it is
written of man, " When he shall die he shall take
nothing away ; nor shall his glory descend with him."

Consequently, my brethren, true riches do not con-
sist in the external goods of fortune, but in the virtues
of the soul, which accompany the conscience to judgment and render us everlastingly wealthy. And with
regard to glory, the Apostle writes, " Our glory is
this, the testimony of our conscience." This indeed
is true glory which comes from the Spirit of truth :
" For the Spirit Himself giveth testimony to our spirit
that we are the sons of God." But the glory which is
given and received amongst men, who " seek not the
glory which is from God alone," that is only vain
glory, because the sons of men are vain. What a fool
thou art who consignest thy money to a sack full of
holes ! who puttest thy treasure in the mouths of men !*
Knowest thou not that this coffer is never closed and
has no lock to secure it ? How much wiser they who

---

* " The glory of men is in their own consciences, not in the
mouths of others."—*Imitation of Christ*, Bk. II. ch. vi.

guard their treasure themselves and refuse to entrust it to others ! But shall they keep it always concealed ? Shall it be hidden for ever ? No, surely not. The time will come when the hidden things of the heart shall be made manifest, and when that which was boastfully exhibited shall no longer appear. Hence it is that at the coming of the Bridegroom the lamps of the foolish virgins go out ; hence too they who receive their reward from men are ignored by Christ. Wherefore I say to you, my dearest brethren, it is much more profitable to hide whatever of good we may seem to possess than to make a public display of it. Thus, when beggars solicit an alms, it is their custom to show, not splendid garments, but half-naked bodies, and sores or ulcers if they have them, in order that the heart of the beholder may more quickly be moved to mercy. This practice was observed much better by the publican of the Gospel than by the Pharisee, and therefore it was that " he went down to his house justified rather than the other."

My brethren, " the time is that judgment should begin at the house of God." What shall be the end of them that obey not the Gospel ? They that rise not in this judgment, what judgment shall they receive ? Let me tell you: all whosoever are unwilling to be judged by this judgment which now is and in which " the prince of this world is cast out," must await or rather must fear the coming of the eternal Judge by Whom they shall themselves be cast out together with their prince. But as for us, let us now judge ourselves strictly, and then securely may " we look for the Saviour, Our Lord Jesus Christ, Who will reform the body of our lowness, made like to the Body of His glory." " Then shall the just shine," those who possessed little learning in this life being now as resplendent in glory as they that had greater ; for they " shall shine as the sun in the kingdom of their Father." But " the light of (that) sun shall be sevenfold, as the light of seven days."

The Saviour, when He comes, " will reform the body of our lowness, made like to the Body of His glory," only on condition, however, that He finds our hearts already reformed and made like to the humility of His own Heart. Therefore has He said, " Learn of Me, because I am meek and humble of Heart." In connection herewith, I would have you take notice, my brethren, that there are two kinds of humility, the one appertaining to knowledge (or to the understanding), the other belonging to the affections (or to the will). It is this latter which Christ calls humility of the heart. By humility of the understanding we know that we are nothing ; and we learn this humility from ourselves and from the experience of our own infirmity. Humility of the will, or of the heart, enables us to trample under foot the glory of the world ; but it is only to be learned from Him Who " emptied Himself, taking the form of a servant," Who fled when the people desired to make Him King, and Who freely offered Himself when they wished to make Him suffer all kinds of ignominy and the shameful death of the cross. Therefore, if we desire to " sleep among the midst of lots," that is to say, if we would rest in security between the two comings of Christ, let our " wings be covered with silver," that is, let us express in our lives that form of the virtues which Christ, when present in the flesh, commended to us both by word and example. For silver may be taken not unreasonably as symbolic of His Human Nature, just as gold is understood to represent His Divinity.

Accordingly, in as far as every virtue of ours falls short of the pattern given us by Christ, in so far does it fall short of true virtue : no wing that we possess is of any worth to bear us aloft unless it be covered with silver. A powerful wing is evangelical poverty, which enables us to fly speedily to the kingdom of heaven. Observe that the other virtues which follow in the Beatitudes obtain only a promise of this kingdom, to be fulfilled at a future time ; but to poverty it is not so much promised as actually given. Hence the reason of the blessedness belonging to the poor is assigned in the present time, " For theirs *is* the kingdom of heaven " ; whereas the future is employed in all the other instances, thus, " Blessed are the meek for they *shall* possess the land," " Blessed are they that mourn for they *shall* be comforted," and so on. But some even of the voluntary poor whom we meet with have not the true poverty beatified by Christ ; because if they had they would not appear so downcast and disconsolate, as being truly kings, aye, kings of heaven. Such are those who desire indeed to be poor, yet on condition that they shall never want for anything ; and they love poverty in such a manner that they will submit to no privation. There are others again who appear to be meek enough so long as there is nothing said or done except what is according to their liking ; but on the slightest occasion, they will show how far they are from true meekness. How can such counterfeit meekness hope to inherit the land, since it does not survive to receive the inheritance ? There are some also whom I see mourning ; but if the tears which flow from their eyes came really from their heart, they would not so easily and so speedily give place to laughter.   As it is, however, whilst idle and jocose words issue forth in greater abundance than did the tears upon which they quickly follow, I cannot believe that it is to such tears the divine consolation has been promised, since unworthy consolation is so soon admitted.   There are others still who manifest such ardent zeal against their neighbour's shortcomings that they might be supposed to " hunger and thirst after justice," if only they appeared to judge their own failings with the same rigorous severity.   But, as a matter of fact, they do not weigh others in the same balance as themselves, and " diverse weights are an abomination before the Lord."   For whilst with equal impudence and futility they are pouring out their anger upon their brother, they are also just as foolishly and just as idly commending themselves.

Some, too, there are who can be very merciful in regard to things with which they have no concern, who are scandalised if all are not abundantly provided for, yet so that they themselves are made to suffer no inconvenience, even the smallest.   Now if such persons would be truly merciful, they ought to exercise mercy at their own expense.   And if they cannot show mercy by giving alms out of their earthly substance, they should at any rate grant pardon with a good will to all who may seem to have offended them.   They should give the pleasant look and the kind word—which is better than any gift—in order to soften the hearts of their enemies and to bring them to repentance.   Moreover, they should give the alms of their compassion and their prayer not only to such as injure them, but

likewise to all whom they know to be in a state of sin ;
otherwise, their mercifulness is a mere pretence, and shall
not avail to obtain mercy.   We may also meet with some
who confess their sins in such a way as to lead one to
think that they are influenced solely by the desire of
purifying their hearts, for confession is a laver in which
all things are made clean.   And yet the fact that they
cannot bear to be accused by others of the very faults
of which they voluntarily accuse themselves shows that
such is not the case.   Were they really as anxious as
they seem to be cleansed of their stains, instead of
feeling irritated, they would rather feel thankful to
those who point out to them their failings.   And finally
there are people who, when they see another scandalised even in the least particular, are filled with anxiety,
studying how they can restore him to peace ; and so
they appear to be peace-makers.   Yet when something
is said or done which seems to give offence to themselves, it takes more time and trouble to calm their
own agitation than that of anybody else.*   But evidently, if they had a true love of peace, they would
seek it for themselves as much as for their neighbours.

Therefore, my brethren, let us silver our wings in
the life of Christ, just as the holy martyrs " have
washed their robes " in the Blood of His passion.   Let
us imitate, as best we can, Him Who loved poverty to
such a degree that, although " in His Hand are all
the ends of the earth," He yet " had not where to
lay His Head," so that the disciples who followed Him
(so we read), as they went through the corn-fields,
compelled by hunger, " plucked the ears and did eat,

* " Thou canst also give good advice and encourage others
with thy words ; but when any unexpected trouble comes to
knock at thy door, then thy counsel and thy courage fail thee."
—*Imitation of Christ*, Bk. III. ch. lvii.

rubbing them in their hands." Let us imitate the meekness of Him Who was "led as a sheep to the slaughter" and was "dumb as a lamb before His shearer and opened not His Mouth." Let us imitate Him Who wept over Lazarus and over Jerusalem, and Who passed whole nights "in the prayer of God," but Who is nowhere said to have laughed or jested.*

Let us imitate Him Who so hungered and thirsted after justice that, although He had no sins of His own, He nevertheless exacted from Himself so terrible a satis-faction for ours, and on the cross thirsted for nothing else but justice. Let us imitate Him Who refused not to die for His enemies, Who prayed for His execu-tioners, Who, though "He did no sin," listened with patience when falsely accused, and Who endured such torments in order to reconcile sinners to Himself.

* Similarly St. John Chrysostom (Homily 14 on 1 Tim.); "Thou laughest and givest thyself up to mirth : thou, who art a monk by profession, who art crucified, who oughtest rather to weep, thou laughest ! Tell me, pray, when did Christ ever act thus ? Thou hast never heard of it, but thou hast often read of His being sad. He wept on beholding Jerusalem, He was troubled at the thought of Judas's treachery, He shed tears when about to call Lazarus from the tomb : and dost thou give way to laughter ? " St. Bernard probably owed his strict views on jesting to the teaching of his master, St. Benedict, who says in chapter vi. of his Rule, " But as to jests (*scurrilitates* = buffoonery) or idle and jocose words, we utterly condemn them, and forbid the brethren to utter a single word of this kind, under any circumstances." Yet the Mellifluous Doctor could appreciate innocent pleasantries. Replying to a facetious epistle sent him by Peter the Venerable, Abbot of Cluny, he says (Ep. ccxxviii.) : " And so thou art pleased to be jocular. Thou art indeed very condescending and sociable. . . . Thy letter was most welcome. I read it with avidity, I read it a second time with renewed pleasure, I read it over and over again and always with fresh delight. The humour (*jocus*), I confess, pleased me very much. It charms by its gracefulness, without offending against decorum. I know not how, with all thy jesting, thou canst still ' dispose thy words in judgment,' so that thy humour detracts nothing from thy dignity, and thy dignity is no obstacle to the sprightliness of thy wit."— (Translator.)

FIFTH SERMON FOR ADVENT

On the second and secret Advent, and how we are to keep the Words of Christ

If any one love Me, he will keep My word, and My Father will love him, and We will come to him, and will make Our abode with him."—John xiv. 23.

In my last sermon I told you, my brethren, that they who have covered their wings with silver must "sleep among the midst of lots." I explained these lots to mean the two advents of Christ, but said nothing concerning the place of sleeping between them. This intermediate place is in fact another advent wherein such as have knowledge thereof enjoy a most pleasant repose. For whereas the other two are known to all, this is secret. In the first "He (Christ) was seen on earth and conversed with men," when, as He Himself bears witness, "they both saw and hated" Him. In the last "all flesh shall see the Salvation of God," and "they shall look on Him Whom they pierced." But in that which intervenes He is hidden, visible only to the elect who see Him in themselves, and so their souls are saved. Therefore, in the first He came in the flesh and in weakness, in the second He comes in spirit and in virtue, and in the third He shall come in glory and majesty. For it is through virtue that glory is reached, as the Psalmist sings, "The Lord of virtues, He is the King of glory." And similarly, the same Prophet says in another place, "In the sanctuary I have come before Thee, to see Thy virtue and Thy

glory." Thus, this intermediate advent is the way, so
to speak, by which we must travel from the first to
the last. In the first Christ was our Redemption, in
the third He shall appear as our Life, whilst in this
second He is our Repose and our Consolation, so that
we may " sleep among the midst of lots."

But perhaps what I have been saying about the
middle advent may seem fanciful to some of you.
Listen, therefore, to the words of Christ Himself, " If
any one love Me, he will keep My words, and My Father
will love him, and We will come to him, and will make
Our abode with him." But how are we to understand
the statement, " If any one love Me, he will keep My
words " ? For I have read elsewhere in Holy Scripture,
" He that feareth God will do good." It appears evident
to me that something greater than this effect of fear is
affirmed of him who loves, when it is said that he will
keep the words of Christ. Where, then, are these
words to be kept ? Doubtless in the heart, as the
Psalmist declares, " Thy words have I hidden in my
heart, that I may not sin against Thee." But in what
manner are they to be kept in the heart ? Shall we
say that it is enough to preserve the memory of them ?
But to those who keep them in this way the Apostle
gives warning that mere " knowledge puffeth up."
Besides, the records of memory are so easily blotted
out by oblivion. Keep the word of God in the same
way in which the food of thy body can be best preserved ; for it is a living bread and the food of thy
soul. Material bread, whilst it is kept in the cupboard
may be stolen by thieves, or nibbled by mice, or may
become stale and unfit for use. But once it has been
assimilated, we have nothing further to fear from such

possibilities. It is thus we should keep the word of God, for " blessed are they who keep it " so. Receive this spiritual bread, therefore, into the stomach of your minds, and having been there properly digested, let it be transmitted thence to the affections and the will. Do not forget (like David) to eat thy bread, lest thy heart (like his) should wither, but nourish thyself therewith that thy soul may be filled " as with marrow and fatness."

My brethren, if you thus keep the word of God, there can be no doubt that it, in turn, shall keep you. For the Son will come to you with the Father, the great Prophet will come to you to rebuild the Jerusalem of your souls and to make all things new. This is the work which the second advent shall accomplish, " that as we have borne the image of the earthly " so may we " bear the image of the heavenly (man)." Just as the old Adam had diffused himself throughout the entire man and had occupied him wholly, in the same way the whole man has passed into the possession of Christ, Who created him wholly, redeemed him wholly, and will glorify him wholly ; for it is He Who " hath made the whole man sound on the Sabbath day." That old man, my brethren, dwelt in us formerly, that ancient prevaricator lived in every one of us ; we had him in our hands, and in our mouths, and in our hearts. He manifested himself through our hands, in two ways, viz., by deeds of violence, and by deeds of shame. In two ways also was he present in our mouths, in arrogant speeches and in words of detraction. And in our hearts similarly his presence was twofold, in carnal desires and in desires of earthly glory. But now for all who have been made new creatures in Christ, " the former things

are passed away." For in their hands innocence has
succeeded to violence, continence to turpitude ; in their
mouths arrogance has given place to humble confession,
detraction to the language of edification, so that, according to the words of Anna, "old matters have
departed from their mouths " ; in their hearts, likewise,
charity has extinguished the desires of the flesh, humility
the love of human greatness. And consider now whether
Christ, the Word of God, is not received according to
these three ways, viz., in the hand, in the mouth, and
in the heart, by each of His elect, to whom He said,
" Put Me as a seal upon thy heart, as a seal upon thy
arm," and in another place, " The Word is nigh thee,
even in thy mouth and in thy heart."

SIXTH SERMON FOR ADVENT

On the Glorification of the Body, and how it must be merited

" *We look for a Saviour, Our Lord Jesus Christ, Who will reform the body of our lowness, made like to the body of His glory.*"
—Phil. iii. 20-21.

Brethren, I would not have you to be in ignorance of the time of your visitation, or of the special object which the Divinity has in view in coming to you now. For the present is the time appointed for attending to the interests, not of the body, but of the soul ; since the soul, being far nobler than the body, has in virtue of this natural superiority the first claim on our solicitude. Besides, that which was the first to fall should also be the first to be raised up. Now it was the soul that, having first brought corruption on herself by sin, brought corruption on the body also as a punishment. Furthermore, if we desire to be found true members of Christ, it is manifest that we must imitate our Head. Hence our first attention must be devoted to the purification of our souls, for the sake of which He has come to us and whose corruption He has first endeavoured to heal. But as for our bodies, let us postpone all concern for these to that time and to that occasion when He shall come again for the purpose of reforming them, as the Apostle assures us, where he says, " We look for the Saviour, Our Lord Jesus Christ, Who will reform the body of our lowness, made like to the Body of His glory." Hence, at the time of the

first coming, St. John Baptist, who seemed to be, and
in truth was, the herald of the Saviour, cried aloud,
" Behold the Lamb of God, behold Him Who taketh
away the sin of the world." Notice how he does not
say " Who taketh away the diseases of the body," or
" the afflictions of the flesh," but, " Who taketh away
sin," which is a malady of the soul and a corruption
of the mind. " Behold Him Who taketh away the sin
of the world." Whence, do you ask ? From the hand,
from the eye, from the neck, even from the flesh itself,
in which it is deeply rooted.

He taketh away sin from our hands, by cleansing us
from the crimes we have committed ; from our eyes,
by purifying the mind's intention ; from our necks, by
removing the galling yoke of spiritual tyranny, according
to what is written, " The yoke of their burden and the
sceptre of their oppressor Thou hast overcome, as in
the day of Madian," and again, " The yoke shall
putrefy at the presence of the oil." And with regard
to the flesh, the Apostle, writing to the Romans, says,
" Let not sin, therefore, reign in your mortal bodies,"
and in another place, " I know that there dwelleth not
in me, that is to say, in my flesh, that which is good,"
and also, " Unhappy man that I am, who shall deliver
me from the body of this death " ? For he knew well
that he could not be without that most baneful root
which is implanted in our flesh, that law of sin which
is in our members, until his soul was separated from
his body, Therefore he desired " to be dissolved
and to be with Christ," knowing that sin, which
" maketh a division between God and us," cannot be
completely taken away so long as we are imprisoned
in the flesh. You have read of one whom the Lord

delivered from the power of the devil, how the demon
went out of him at the divine command, casting him
down and " greatly tearing him." I say to you, that
this kind of sin—I mean carnal appetites and evil
desires which so often assail us—can indeed and ought
to be kept down by the grace of God, so far as this,
that it shall not reign in us, and that we shall not
yield our members unto it " as instruments of iniquity,"—and so there shall be " no condemnation to
them that are in Christ Jesus " ; but that it cannot
be cast out except by death, when we shall be so
" greatly torn " that our souls shall be parted from our
bodies.

I have now explained to you, my brethren, the
purpose of Christ's coming, and I have told you what
should be the great object of the Christian's solicitude.
Wherefore, do not, O body, do not, I pray thee, anti-
cipate thy time. For although thou hast the power to
hinder the salvation of the soul, thou canst do absolutely nothing to secure thine own. " All things have
their season," as the Wise Man says. Permit the
soul now to work for her own interests, or rather
do thou co-operate with her, because if thou sufferest
with her, thou shalt also reign with her. On the
other hand, by impeding her restoration thou wouldst
be impeding thine own in the same proportion. For
thou canst not be perfected until the Creator beholds
His image restored in her. O mortal flesh, noble
is the guest whom thou art entertaining, yea, very
noble, and on her welfare thine own entirely depends.
Honour thy guest so distinguished. Thou art residing
here in thy native country, but the soul, which
has taken lodging with thee, is a pilgrim and an

exile on the earth. Where, I ask thee, is the peasant who, if some powerful nobleman wished to spend the night under his roof, would not gladly (as is only proper) place his best bed at the service of his guest even though he should himself have to sleep in some corner of the house, under the stairs, or on the very hearth-stone? Therefore, "go and do thou in like manner." Do not consider the sufferings and inconveniences thou mayest have to endure, provided thy guest can be honourably lodged with thee. Esteem it as thy greatest honour to be stripped of all honour in this life for the sake of the soul.

And lest thou shouldst perhaps feel tempted to despise or to undervalue this guest of thine, for that she seems to thee a stranger and a pilgrim, consider diligently the many precious advantages which thou owest to her presence. For it is she that gives sight to thine eyes and hearing to thine ears; it is from her thy tongue borrows its power of speech, thy palate its discernment of taste, and all thy members their various motions. Whatever of life, whatever of sense or feeling, whatever of beauty thou possessest in thyself, know that it is all the benefit of thy guest. It is only her departure from thee that will show how much thou owest to her presence. For as soon as the soul withdraws, the tongue shall be silent, the eyes shall become blind, the ears shall lose their hearing, pallor shall overspread the countenance, the whole body shall grow rigid, and after a brief interval shall be changed into a sink of corruption, all its beauty being converted to rottenness. And wilt thou, then, O body, wound and grieve this guest for the sake of any temporal delight whatever, which thou couldst not even enjoy except

through her ? Besides, if even now, in the time of her
banishment, when exiled for her sins from the presence
of her Maker, she bestows upon thee such a multitude
of benefits, what shall she not do for thee, after she
has been restored to favour ? Be careful, then, oh,
be careful not to hinder that reconciliation, since from
it thou shalt thyself derive a generous endowment of
glory. Expose thyself with patience, nay, with gladness, to all kinds of sufferings and privations. Refuse
no sacrifice which may seem to conduce to so happy a
restoration. Speak to thy guest in the words of
Joseph to his fellow-captive, " The Lord will remember
thee and will restore thee to thy former place. Only
remember me when it shall be well with thee."

Yes, she will undoubtedly be mindful to render thee
good, if meanwhile thou dost faithfully serve her. And
when she comes into the presence of her Lord, she will
speak to Him of thee. Out of gratitude for thy hos-
pitality she will plead thy cause with Him, saying,
" When Thy servant was an exile, in punishment for
her sin, a poor fellow-servant with whom I lodged
treated me with great kindness, and I pray that my
Lord may be pleased to make him a return in my
behalf. For, in the first place, he sacrificed all he possessed in my service, and then his very self, not sparing
anything of his own, in order to further my interests,
' in labour and painfulness, in much watchings, in
hunger and thirst, in fastings often, in cold and naked-
ness.' " What, then, will the Lord do ? Surely, the
Scripture does not lie when it says, " He will do the
will of them that fear Him and He will hear their
prayer." Oh, if thou couldst only taste this sweetness,
if only thou couldst conceive this glory whereof I am

about to speak! For what I shall say is in very truth strange and astonishing, yet none the less certain and indubitable to faithful souls. He Himself, the Lord God of Sabaoth, the Lord of Hosts and the King of Glory, He will Himself come down to reform our bodies and to make them like to the Body of His brightness! Oh, how great shall be that glory, how unspeakable that exultation, when the Creator of the universe, Who before came hidden and humble for the purpose of justifying souls, comes now visible and sublime to glorify thee, O flesh, so poor at present and so miserable; comes not in weakness as of old, but in all the splendour of His Majesty! "Who shall be able to think of the day of (this) coming" of the Lord, when He will descend in the fulness of His glory, preceded by the angels, who with the sound of the trumpet shall "raise up the needy (body) from the dust," "taking it up together with them into the clouds to meet Christ, into the air."

Shall we therefore continue to allow this flesh of ours, this miserable, foolish, blind, and senseless flesh, this utterly infatuated flesh, to seek after earthly and transitory consolations, or rather desolations, with the risk of being rejected and judged unworthy of that glory, and of being condemned besides to suffer inexpressible torments for all eternity? Let it not be so, I beseech you, brethren, let it not be so. Rather let our spirits find their delight in holy meditations, and let our flesh rest in hope, whilst "we look for the Saviour, Our Lord Jesus Christ, Who will reform the body of our lowness, made like to the Body of His glory." For so the Psalmist sings, "For Thee my soul hath thirsted, for Thee my flesh, oh, how many ways!"

Thus did the soul of the Royal Prophet yearn for the first advent, whereby she knew that she was to be redeemed ; and with much greater eagerness did his flesh look forward to the final coming, at which shall be accomplished its glorification. For then all our desires shall be satisfied, and the whole earth shall be filled with the Majesty of the Lord. To this glory, to this happiness, to this " peace which surpasseth all understanding," may He bring us by His mercy and not " confound us in our expectation," the Saviour Whom we look for, Jesus Christ Our Lord, Who is over all things, God blessed for ever. Amen.

SEVENTH SERMON FOR ADVENT

ON OUR THREEFOLD NEED OF CHRIST

" If God be for us, who is against us ? "—Rom. viii. 31.

My brethren, if we celebrate with devotion the
advent of the Lord, we are doing nothing more than
our duty, because not only has He come to us, but He
has come also for our sakes, He Who " hath no need
of our goods." Yea, rather it was our need of Him
that induced Him to visit us, and the greatness of that
need is clearly indicated by the greatness of His condescension. And just as the gravity of the disease may
be inferred from the costliness of the medicine employed for its cure, so too may we ascertain the number
of our ailments from the multitude of the remedies
provided for us. For wherefore the " divisions of
graces," unless they correspond to a variety of necessities ? It would be a difficult undertaking to attempt
to discuss in one sermon all the spiritual wants which
we experience ; but there are three which now occur
to my mind, which are common to all, and which may
be regarded as the principal. For there is not a soul
amongst us that does not sometimes feel the need of
counsel, of help, and of protection. It is indubitable that the whole human race labours under a
threefold misery, a triple burden, which painfully
oppresses every man so long as he lives in this region
of the shadow of death, subject to the infirmities of the
flesh and the assaults of temptation. For we are easily

led astray ; we soon weary of labour ; we quickly yield to violence. We are deceived when we try to discern between good and evil ; we faint and give up as often as we undertake a good work ; if we endeavour to resist evil, we are promptly cast down and overcome.

Very necessary, therefore, is the advent of the Saviour ; very necessary is the presence of Christ to men so encompassed with dangers. God grant that He may not only come to us, but that He may also in His infinite mercy dwell in us by faith to illumine our blindness ; remain with us by His grace to assist our utter impotence ; and stand by us with His power to protect and defend our fragility ! For if He dwells in us, who shall seduce us ? If He remains with us, surely we " can do all things in Him Who strengtheneth" us. If He " be for us who is against us " ? He is a faithful Counsellor, Who never can deceive us or be deceived ; He is a strong Helper, Whom labour never wearies ; He is a mighty Protector, Who will speedily enable us to trample under foot the power of Satan and will bring to naught all his cunning machinations. For He is the Wisdom of God, Who is ever ready to instruct the ignorant ; and He is the Power of God, to Whom it is easy to strengthen the fainting and to rescue the perishing. Therefore, my brethren, in all doubts and perplexities, let us have recourse to so wise a Master ; in all our undertakings, let us invoke the assistance of so powerful a Helper ; in our every combat let us commit our souls to the keeping of so faithful a Protector, Who for this purpose has come into the world, that, living here in men, with men, and for men, He may illuminate their darkness, lighten their labours, and guard them from all danger. Amen.

SERMONS FOR CHRISTMAS EVE

FIRST SERMON FOR CHRISTMAS EVE

On the three Benefits which we owe to the Birth of Christ

" Jesus Christ, the Son of God, is born in Bethlehem of Juda."*

The voice of joy has been heard in our land, " the voice of rejoicing and salvation in the tabernacles " not " of the just," however, but of sinners. We have heard the " good word " the " consoling word," the word full of sweetness and " worthy of all acceptation." " Ye mountains, give praise with jubilation," and let " all the trees of the forest clap their hands " " before the face of the Lord because He cometh." " Hear, O ye heavens, and give ear, O earth." Let every creature, but especially thou, O man, be astonished and give praise to the Lord, because " Jesus Christ, the Son of God, is born in Bethlehem of Juda." Oh, what heart can be so flinty, what soul so insensible, as not to melt with love at hearing this announcement? What sweeter tidings could be published? What happier event could be proclaimed? Has the world ever before heard anything like this, or has news like this been ever told? " Jesus Christ, the Son of God, is born in Bethlehem of Juda." O short word of the " shortened Word," but full of heavenly sweetness! Truly love is here in labour, eager to pour out more

---

* These words are taken from the announcement of Christmas in the Cistercian Martyrology.—(Translator.)

plentifully the abundance of its mellifluous tenderness, and unable to find more adequate expression. For so perfect is the beauty and charm of this short verse that you cannot change a single iota without spoiling it. " Jesus Christ, the Son of God, is born in Bethlehem of Juda." O nativity spotless in sanctity, glory of the world, dear to man by reason of the greatness of the benefit it confers, inscrutable even to the angels because of the depth of its divine mystery, admirable to all in its novelty and unparalleled excellence ! Nativity, which, to borrow the words of the Poet :

> " Had no precursor in the years before,
> And peerless shall remain for evermore." *

O birth of Christ, alone unaccompanied by pain, alone pure and immaculate, not violating but consecrating the Mother's integrity ! O nativity, beyond nature, yet designed for the good of nature ; transcending nature by thy miraculous excellence, restoring nature by the power of thy mystery ! My brethren, " who shall declare (this) generation ? " The Angel announces it, the power of the Most High overshadows it, the Holy Ghost descends upon it. A virgin believes, a virgin conceives by her faith, she brings forth as a virgin, and remains ever a virgin. Who can help wondering at all this ? The Son of the Most High is born : God of God, begotten before the ages, is born to-day as a speechless Babe ! Who can now wonder sufficiently ?

And this nativity has not been in vain, not in vain has been the condescension of the Divine Majesty.

---

* " Nec primam similem visa est, nec habere sequentem."— The Irish poet Sedulius, *Carmen Paschale*, iii. 39, who is here speaking of the Blessed Virgin. —(Translator.)

" Jesus Christ, the Son of God, is born in Bethlehem
of Juda." " Awake and give praise, ye that dwell
in the dust." Behold the Lord cometh with salvation,
He cometh with ointments, He cometh with glory.
For Jesus cometh not without salvation, nor Christ
without unction, nor without glory the Son of God,
Who is Himself Salvation and Unction, Who is Himself Glory, according to what is written, " A wise son
is the glory of his father." Happy the soul, which
after tasting the fruit of His salvation, runs to the
odour of His ointments, in order that she may · see
His glory, " the glory as it were of the Only-Begotten
of the Father." Take courage all ye who have wandered
away, because Jesus comes to seek and to save that
which was lost. Ye that are sick be of good cheer,
for Christ has come to anoint the contrite of heart
with the unction of His mercy. Exult and be glad,
ye who are ambitious of glory, since the Son of God
has descended to you to make you co-heirs of His
kingdom. Thus, O Lord, thus, I pray Thee, " heal
me and I shall be healed ; save me and I shall be
saved," glorify me and I shall be glorious. Then shall
I say with the Psalmist, " Bless the Lord, O my soul,
and let all that is within me bless His holy name.
Bless the Lord, O my soul, and never forget all He
hath done for thee, Who forgiveth all thy iniquities,
Who healeth all thy infirmities, Who satisfieth thy desire
with good things." As for me, my dearest brethren,
I experience from these three things a threefold savour
of sweetness in the announcement that " Jesus Christ,
the Son of God, is born." For why do we call His
name Jesus unless because " He shall save His people
from their sins ? " And why has He willed to be

called Christ, unless because He " shall make the yoke to putrify at the presence of the oil ? " And wherefore has the Son of God made Himself the Son of man if it be not to make men the sons of God ? Who shall oppose His will ? It is Jesus " That justifieth, who is he that shall condemn ? " It is Christ That healeth, who is he that shall hurt ? It is the Son of God That raiseth us up, who is he that shall cast us down ?

Jesus is born : oh, rejoice all ye whomsoever the consciousness of sin foredooms to everlasting damnation ! For the mercy of Jesus is greater than any degree of malice, greater than any number of crimes. Christ is born : let gladness arise in every soul which is struggling with long-established habits of evil. For no spiritual malady, no matter how inveterate, shall be able to stand before the face of the unction of Christ. The Son of God is born : exult thou who art wont to aspire to greatness, because the Giver of great rewards is at hand. My brethren, " this is the Heir," let us lovingly receive Him, " that the inheritance may be ours." For He Who hath given us His cwn Son, " how hath He not also with Him given us all things ? " Let no one disbelieve it, let no one doubt it, for we are assured by a most trustworthy witness that " the Word was made flesh and dwelt amongst us." The only-begotten Son of God willed to share His sonship with us, " that He might be the First-Born among many brethren." And in order that weak and pusillanimous mortals might be left no excuse for doubting this, He first made Himself the Brother of man, and the Son of man, by truly taking upon Him our human nature.

" Jesus Christ, the Son of God, is born in Bethlehem of Juda." Notice the humility exhibited in the choice

of place. Not in Jerusalem, the city of the kings, is
He born, but in Bethlehem, which is but " a little one
among the thousands of Juda." O Bethlehem, here-
tofore little indeed, but now magnified by the Lord !
Thou hast been made great by Him Who in thee has
made Himself little from great. Exult, O Bethlehem,
and through all thy streets let joyous alleluias be sung
to-day ! What city that ever hears of it will not
envy thee that most venerable stable and the glory
of that poor manger ! Thy name is now famous
throughout the whole world, and " all generations
shall call (thee) blessed." Everywhere, " glorious
things are said of thee, O city of God." Everywhere
resounds the song of joy : " A Man is born in her and
the Same hath founded her, the Most High."* Everywhere, I say, it is preached and proclaimed that " Jesus
Christ, the Son of God, is born in Bethlehem of Juda."
And not without purpose is the addition of the words,
" of Juda," by which we are reminded of the promise
made to the fathers by the mouth of the Patriarch

---

* " Numquid Sion dicet homo : et homo natus est in ea et
Ipse fundavit eam Altissimus ? " (Ps. lxxxvi. 5). It was thus
St. Bernard and nearly all the Latin Fathers read this verse;
not as it is now written : " Numquid Sion dicet : Homo et homo
natus est in ea, et Ipse fundavit eam Altissimus ? " which the
Douay Translators render, " Shall not Sion say : This man
and that man is born in her ? and the Highest Himself hath
founded her." But this is at variance with the Hebrew in
which Sion is dative case, not nominative, and besides differs
in gender from the verb. Moreover, the modern reading seems
to make hardly any sense, whilst the patristic contains a pro-
phecy of the Incarnation, and so this verse was much used
by the early Christian apologists. The Greek has : " μήτηρ
Σιὼν ἐρεῖ ἄνθρωπος, καὶ ἄνθρωπος ἐγενήθη ἐν αὐτῇ, καὶ αὐτὸς
ἐθεμελίωσεν αὐτὴν ὁ ὕψιστος." This also appears to be unintelligible. But St. Jerome declares that the word " μήτηρ "
(mother) was substituted by mistake for " μήτι " (numquid).
Cf. Bellarmin.—(Translator).

Jacob, " The sceptre shall not be taken away from Juda nor a ruler from his thigh till He come That is to be sent, and He shall be the expectation of nations." For though " salvation is of the Jews," yet it reaches " to the farthest parts of the earth." And the same Patriarch also prophesied, " Juda, thee shall thy brethren praise ; thy hands shall be upon the necks of thy enemies." These and other predictions which are nowhere recorded to have been verified of the typical Juda, we now see fulfilled in Christ. For He is " the Lion of the tribe of Juda," of Whom it is added, " Juda is a lion's whelp : to the prey, my Son, Thou art gone up." A mighty Spoiler is Christ, Who " before He knew to call His Father and Mother carried off the spoils of Samaria." Christ is indeed a mighty Spoiler, Who " ascending on high, led captivity captive." He did not, however, take away anything from us, but rather " gave gifts to men." In this way, therefore, these and similar prophecies, which we perceive to be fulfilled in Christ, (of Whom also they were spoken), are recalled to our minds when we hear the announcement, " Jesus Christ, the Son of God, is born in Bethlehem of Juda." And there is no longer any necessity for us to inquire whether anything of good can come from Bethlehem.

As to what concerns us, my brethren, we learn how He desires to be received from the fact that He chose Bethlehem for His birthplace. Perhaps there were then some who thought that a magnificent palace should be made ready in which the King of glory might be honourably entertained. But it was not for earthly honour that the " almighty Word leapt down from heaven from (His) royal throne," where " length of days is in (His) Right Hand, and in (His) Left Hand riches and glory." He possessed from everlasting an inexhaustible store of all such things in heaven. One treasure, however, He could not find there, namely, the treasure of poverty, of which there was on earth an abundance and a superabundance, although man had no suspicion of its worth. It was, therefore, for the sake of this that the Son of God came down from His throne on high, in order to choose it for Himself and by His appreciation to teach us its value. Adorn, then, O Sion, adorn thy bridal couch : but let it be with the ornaments of poverty and humility. These are the swathing-clothes which please Him best ; these, as Mary bears witness, are the silks wherewith He delights to be clothed. Let us, therefore, " sacrifice the abominations of the Egyptians to the Lord our God."

Consider lastly, my brethren, that it is in Bethlehem of Juda Jesus is born, and study how each one of you may make himself a Bethlehem of Juda, for thus He will not disdain to be born in you also. Now Bethlehem means " the house of bread," and Juda signifies " praise " or " confession." Consequently, if thou fillest thy soul with the food of holy doctrine ; if also thou faithfully and with all possible devotion—unworthy though it must ever be—receive that Living Bread " Which cometh down from heaven and giveth life to the world " (I mean the Body of the Lord Jesus) so that His glorified Flesh may repair and strengthen the " old bottle " of thy body, which thus fortified shall be able to hold the new wine poured into it ; if, finally, thou livest by faith and art never obliged to avow with tears that thou hast " forgotten to eat thy bread ": thou art now become a Bethlehem, and comparatively fit to receive the Lord, if yet confession be not wanting. Then let " Judæa be thy sanctification," "put on praise and beauty," the robes wherewith Christ would have His ministers clothed. The Apostle, lastly, commends these two things very briefly where he says, " With the heart we believe unto justice and with the mouth confession is made unto salvation." For justice in the heart is as bread in the house. That justice may be called bread is clear from the words of Christ, " Blessed are they that hunger and thirst after justice, for they shall have their fill." Let justice, therefore, be in thy heart, the justice which is of faith, for this alone "hath glory before God." In thy mouth also have the confession which "is made unto salvation : " so shalt thou be able to receive with confidence Him Who is born in Bethlehem of Juda, Jesus Christ, the Son of God.

SECOND SERMON FOR CHRISTMAS EVE

On the Spiritual Jews and the Spiritual Jerusalem, and the Desire which all the Blessed feel for our Salvation

" O Juda and Jerusalem, fear ye not and be ye not dismayed :
to-morrow you shall go out and the Lord will be with you."
—II Par. xx. 17.

My brethren, I am here addressing the true Israelites, those who are Jews not according to the letter, but according to the spirit : the true seed of Abraham which we now behold multiplied in fulfilment of the promise we have read of in Genesis. For " not they that are the children of the flesh, but they that are the children of the promise, are accounted for the seed." And the Jerusalem to which I speak is not the Jerusalem that killed the prophets. For what consolation could I offer the city over which Christ wept and which has been given up to destruction ? But as it is to the spiritual Jews, so also is it to the spiritual Jerusalem (which has come down new out of heaven) that I say, " O Juda and Jerusalem, fear ye not." Fear not, ye true confessors,* who confess to the Lord not alone with your mouths, but with all your members and faculties, and with your whole being, having " put on confession " as a garment ; who glorify Him with all your vitals and all whose bones exclaim, " Lord, who is like to Thee ? "—very different from those who " confess that

---

* In the preceding sermon the holy Preacher mentioned that the word Juda signifies " confession," hence the true Jews are true confessors.—(Translator.)

they know God, but in their deeds deny Him." Your
confession, my brethren, is then true and perfect when
all your works are the works of God and all contribute
to His glory. But let your confession be twofold,
in order that you may be clothed in " double garments."
I mean to say, you ought to unite the confession of
your sins with the confession of the divine praises.
For then you shall be Jews indeed if your whole life
is a confession that you are sinners, deserving of much
greater chastisement than you have received, and
that God is the sovereign Goodness, Who commutes
to the trivial and transitory sufferings of this life the
everlasting punishment you have deserved. But he
who has not an eager desire for penance seems to say
by his conduct either that he has no need of penance,
and so he refuses to confess his sins, or that penance
is for him of no avail, and so he does not confess the
divine goodness. Be ye, however, true Jews, be ye
also the true Jerusalem, that so you may have nothing
to fear. For Jerusalem means " the vision of peace,"
the vision (not the possession) whose " ends " (not
whose beginning or whose middle) the Lord " hath
disposed in peace." If therefore you have not peace,
rather because you cannot have perfect peace in this
world, at least gaze upon it, contemplate it, think
of it, long for it. Let the eyes of your heart and the
intention of your mind be ever directed towards peace,
so that all your actions may be performed from the
desire of the peace " which surpasseth all understanding." Let this be your aim in everything you
do, that, being reconciled, " you may have peace
with God."

It is to persons of such disposition I say, " Fear

ye not," it is to these I offer consolation, not to those
who "have not known the way of peace." For were
I to say to them, "To-morrow you shall go out,"
I should appear rather to threaten than to console.
They alone who have the vision of peace and who
"know if their earthly house of this habitation be
dissolved, that they have a building of God, a house
not made with hands, eternal in heaven," they alone,
I say, "desire to be dissolved" and are eager to "go
out," not like those others who, as if afflicted with in-
sanity, take pleasure in their bondage. For of the
latter it would be more true to say that they go in when
they die than that they "go out," because they go not
out to light and liberty, but rather go in to darkness,
to prison, and to hell. But to you, my brethren, I may
truly say, "Fear ye not and be ye not dismayed;
to-morrow you shall go out," and there shall be no
alarm in your confines. You have indeed many
antagonists: the flesh, which is the most domestic of
all enemies; the present wicked world, by which you
are surrounded; and the princes of darkness, who
live in the air and lie in wait to surprise you. Nevertheless, "fear ye not and be ye not dismayed;
to-morrow you shall go out." That is to say, you
shall go out on the day after this, because to-morrow
signifies next day. Thus the holy Patriarch Jacob said,
"My justice shall answer for me to-morrow." There are,
my brethren, three spiritual days, whereof it is written
in the Prophet Osee, "He will receive us after two
days, and on the third day He will raise us up." The
first of these days is the day under Adam, the second
the day in Christ, and the third the day with Christ.
Hence the same Prophet continues, "We shall know,

and we shall follow on, that we may know the Lord ":
and here it is said, "To-morrow you shall go out and
the Lord will be with you." For these words are
addressed to those who "have shortened (dimidiave-
runt) their days," for whom has perished the day
in which they were born, which is the day of Adam,
the day of sin, the day cursed by Jeremias, who said,
"Cursed be the day wherein I was born." We have
all of us been born in that day. And God grant that
it may perish for us also, that day of mists and clouds,
that day of darkness and storm, the day which we
owe to Adam, which we owe to the enemy, who seduced
him with the promise that his eyes should be opened.

But behold the new day of redemption has dawned
upon us, the day of reparation of the ancient fall, the
day of everlasting felicity. "This is the day which the
Lord hath made : let us be glad and rejoice therein,"
because "to-morrow (we) shall go out." And whence
shall we go out, except from the confinement of this
world, from the prison of this body, from the fetters
of corporal necessity, of curiosity, vanity, and pleasure,
which, even in spite of us, hold fast the feet of our
affection ? For what has our spirit in common with
the creatures of earth ? Why does it not desire
spiritual things ? why not seek after spiritual things ?
why not relish spiritual things ? O spirit of man,
whose home is on high, what hast thou to do with
the things below ? "Seek the things that are above,
where Christ is sitting at the Right Hand of God ;
mind the things that are above, not the things that
are upon the earth." But alas ! "the corruptible
body is a load upon the soul, and the earthly habitation presseth down the mind that museth upon many

things." The numerous necessities of this wretched body hold us back. The fascination of evil desires and worldly pleasures is as bird-lime to our souls, preventing their flight to heaven, yea, and it quickly drags them down again, if ever they should chance to soar aloft. Yet, " fear ye not and be ye not dismayed : to-morrow you shall go out," " out of the pit of misery and the mire of dregs." For in order to draw you forth thence, Christ first allowed Himself to " stick fast in the mire of the deep." Therefore, " fear ye not and be ye not dismayed : to-morrow you shall go out " of " the body of this death " and of all the corruption of sin. Spend this day in Christ, so that you also may walk even as He walked. For " he that saith he abideth in Him ought himself also to walk even as He walked." " Fear ye not," therefore, " and be ye not dismayed ; to-morrow you shall go out," " and so shall (you) be always with the Lord." But perhaps from the fact that it is said expressly : " and the Lord will be with you," we are to infer that, whilst we live here below, it is possible for us to be with the Lord, viz., by being conformed to His will, although He may not be with us so as to consent to our desires. For we should be glad to be now at liberty, we wish to be at once dissolved, we are impatient to " go out " ; but He, for some secret cause, still defers to gratify our longing. However, " to-morrow we shall go out, and the Lord will be with us," in such a way that our pleasure shall be His pleasure, and there shall be no longer the least opposition, but the most perfect harmony between His will and ours.

Therefore I say, " Juda and Jerusalem, fear ye not

and be ye not dismayed " if you have not yet attained to that degree of virtue which you desire. Let the humility of your confession make up for what is wanting to the perfection of your lives, because, as the Psalmist says of himself to God, " Thy eyes have seen my imperfection." For the reason why the Lord has commanded His " commandments to be kept most diligently" is in order that men, made sensible of their shortcomings, and realising their insufficiency to fulfil what is enjoined, may have recourse to the divine mercy, saying with holy David, " Thy mercy is better than lives." Thus, since they are unable to clothe themselves in the garments of justice and innocence, they should at least appear vested in the humility of confession. For " confession and beauty are before Him," that is to say, find favour in His eyes, if yet (as I have already remarked) it be not the confession of the mouth only, but of the whole man, so that all our bones shall exclaim, " Lord, who is like to Thee ? " —and this with a view to peace alone, and from the sole desire of being reconciled to God. It is only to such are addressed the words, " O Juda and Jerusalem, fear ye not and be ye not dismayed : to-morrow you shall go out." That is to say, as soon as the soul parts from the body, all the desires and affections by which she is now attached to earthly objects and drawn around the world, shall be entirely dissolved, so that, freed from this bondage, she " shall go out and the Lord will be with " her. Such happiness may indeed seem excessive to you if you consider only yourselves, and look not to the " expectation of the creature " which " waiteth for the revelation of the sons of God." Does not the whole universe look forward to this

consummation ?   " For the creature was made subject
to vanity"; when, on the fall of man, whom the Lord
had " made master of His house and ruler of all His
possession," his whole inheritance participated in his
corruption.   As a consequence, the air was deprived
of its original temperateness; the earth was cursed
in the works of man, and vanity was given power
over all earthly creatures.

Nor shall the inheritance be renewed until the heir
has been first restored.   Hence, according to the testimony of the Apostle, " it groaneth and travaileth in
pain even till now."   And " we are made a spectacle,"
not only " to the world " but also " to angels and
to men."   Hence the Psalmist says to God, " The
just wait for me until Thou reward me."   And when
the martyrs prayed for the day of judgment—not
from any desire of vengeance, but because they long
for the perfection of happiness which they shall then
obtain*—they received the divine answer bidding them
to " rest for a little time till their fellow-servants and

---

* The holy Preacher here insinuates what he openly teaches
elsewhere (*De dilig. Deo*, xi. ; *De Consid.*, v. 4 ; Serm. i. and iii.,
de omnibus sanctis), namely, that the souls of the saints, are
although they are in heaven and enjoy the Beatific Vision, are
not yet perfectly united to God by love, nor (by consequence)
perfectly happy, so long as they are separated from their bodies.
This is the view in which St. Augustine appears to have finally
rested, after repeatedly affirming that the just souls are not
admitted to the Beatific Vision at all before the General
Judgment (*De Civit. Dei*, xii. 9 ; In Joan., 49 ; Retract., i. 14).
The Angelic Doctor at first followed St. Bernard, but afterwards
changed his mind, and taught that the reunion with the flesh
shall increase the soul's happiness, not " intensivè," but only
" extensivè."   This is the opinion now generally received ; but
the question has never been decided dogmatically.   For the
Canon of the Council of Florence (1438) stating that " the souls
of the saints are now perfectly happy, but shall have greater
happiness after the Resurrection," may be and has been
interpreted in favour of both views.—(Translator.)

their brethren, who are to be slain, even as they, shall be filled up." They have already received each a single robe ; but they shall not be clothed in double garments until we also shall be clothed with them. We even hold as pledges and hostages their sacred bodies, without which they cannot be consummated, nor shall they be restored to them without us. Therefore the Apostle says of the patriarchs and prophets, " All these, being approved by the testimony of faith, receive not the promise, God providing some better thing for us, that they should not be perfected without us." Oh, if we only knew with what eagerness they await, with what ardour they desire our coming ! how earnestly they seek and how gladly they hear whatever conduces to our spiritual welfare !

But why do I speak of those who have learned compassion from the things which they suffered, since even the holy angels long for our advent ? Worms though we are and vilest dust, yet is it not with us as with living stones that the walls of the heavenly Jerusalem have to be repaired ? And with what eagerness, think you, do these citizens of paradise yearn to see the integrity of their city restored ? Oh, how anxiously do they await the arrival of the rational stones with which the fissures in their wall shall be built up ! How they speed to and fro between God and us, most faithfully representing our groans to Him, and most lovingly bearing back to us His graces ! Assuredly they will not disdain to recognise us as their associates seeing that already they minister to us as our servants. For " are they not all ministering spirits, sent to minister for them who shall receive the inheritance of salvation ? " Let us hasten, therefore, my dearest brethren, let us hasten, I pray you. The whole multitude of the heavenly host are awaiting us. We made the angels rejoice when we were converted to penance ; let us go forward, let us make haste to perfect the joy which our happiness causes them. Woe to thee, whosoever thou art, that wouldst wallow again in the mire and go back to the vomit ! Dost thou expect to have them propitious to thee at the judgment whom thou art now disposed to defraud of a joy so great and so ardently longed for ? They were filled with gladness when we gave ourselves up to penance ; they exulted over us, because they saw us returning, so to speak, from the very mouth of hell. What now shall be their feelings if they behold us turning away from the portals of paradise and going back, after placing one foot in heaven ? For the heart may dwell in heaven even though the body abides on the earth.

Make haste, then, my brethren, make haste, I say, because not the angels only, but the Creator of the angels Himself is awaiting you. " The marriage indeed is ready," but the house is not yet full. There are others still awaited in order that " the marriage may be filled with guests." God the Father is looking out for you with yearning, not alone " for His exceeding charity wherewith He hath loved us," as the Apostle bears witness (and " the only-begotten Son, Who is in the Bosom of the Father, He likewise hath declared " it, saying : " The Father Himself loveth you ") but also for His own sake, as He tells us by His Prophet, " It is not for your sake I will do this, O house of Israel, but for My holy name's sake." For who can doubt the fulfilment of the promise which He (the

Father has made to His Son in the words, "Ask of Me
and I will give Thee the gentiles for Thy inheritance"?
And elsewhere He says, " Sit Thou at My Right Hand,
until I make Thy enemies Thy footstool." Now all
Christ's enemies have not been crushed so long as they
continue their attacks upon us who are His members.
Nor shall the promise be entirely fulfilled until death,
the last of our enemies, has been utterly destroyed.
And as concerns the Son, who does not know how
much He desires " the fruit of (His) nativity," the
fruit of the whole life which He lived in the flesh, the
fruit of His cross and of His death, the price of His
most precious Blood? Is He not to deliver up the
kingdom which He has acquired " to God and the
Father "? Is He not to restore to the Father those
creatures of His for the sake of whom He was sent
down to the earth? And the Holy Spirit also expects
us. For He is the Charity and the Benignity of God,
and it is in Him we have been predestined from everlasting. Surely then we cannot doubt that He desires
to see that predestination accomplished.

Therefore, my brethren, since all the court of heaven
desires and expects us, let us " run not as at an un-
certainty." Let us run by holy desires and by our
progress in virtue. For to grow in sanctity is to hasten
forward. Let each one of us repeat with the Psalmist,
" Look upon me and have mercy on me, according
to the judgment of them that love Thy name." That
is to say, " Show me mercy, not according to my
deserts, but according to the good will of them that
love Thee truly." Let us also repeat with Judas
Machabeus, " As it shall be the will of God in heaven
so be it done," and with the Lord Himself, " Thy

will be done on earth as it is in heaven." For we
know that it is written, " If God be for us, who is
against us ? " Also, "who shall accuse against the
elect of God ? " And " Is it not lawful for Me to do
what I will ? " Therefore, dearest brethren, let this
be your consolation in the meantime until " you shall
go out and the Lord will be with you." To which
happy going out may He in His great mercy lead us,
and to that glorious to-morrow. And on this nearer
to-morrow also may He vouchsafe to visit us and to
remain with us, so that if any one amongst us happens
to be held captive by some temptation, he may " go
out " therefrom to-morrow, through the grace of
Him who cometh to " preach a deliverance to them
that are shut up," and that with a holy gladness we
may receive the crown of joy from the Hand of our
new-born King, Who with the Father and the Holy
Ghost liveth and reigneth one God for ever and ever.
Amen.

THIRD SERMON FOR CHRISTMAS EVE

On the Three Days, the Three Watches, the Three Winds, and the Three Unions

*" To-day you shall know that the Lord will come and in the morning you shall see the glory of the Lord." *—*Exod. xvi. 6-7.

Oh, " all you that are earth-born and ye sons of men," " awake and give praise, ye that dwell in the dust," because the Physician is coming to the sick, the Redeemer to the captives, the Way to the wanderers, Life to the dead ; because He is coming Who " will cast all our sins into the bottom of the sea," Who will " heal all our diseases," and will bear us back upon His own shoulders to the place of honour which originally was ours. This no doubt, is an exercise of great power. But far more wonderful is the mercy therein displayed : that He who is able to succour us should be willing thus to come. " To-day you shall know that the Lord will come." These words, my brethren, have been set down in Holy Scripture in their proper place and order as relating to an event of an earlier time; yet not unappropriately are they addressed to

---

* This seems to be only an adaptation of Exodus xvi. 6–7, where the Vulgate has, " In the evening you shall know that the Lord hath brought you forth out of the land of Egypt, and in the morning you shall see the glory of the Lord." But the text as given by St. Bernard is found also in the Introit of the Mass of Christmas Eve, and in the office for the day.— (Translator.)

72

us by mother Church on the vigil of the Lord's nativity. For the Church is guided by the counsel and by the Spirit of Him Who is at once her Bridegroom and her God. She has the Beloved " abiding between her breasts," guarding her heart for Himself, and occupying it like a king upon his throne. She is the Spouse who has wounded His Heart, who with the eye of contemplation pierces the abyss of God's hidden designs, and so makes an everlasting dwelling for herself in His Heart and for Him in her own. Whenever, therefore, she changes the meaning or the application of a text of Holy Scripture, the words in the accommodated sense possess even greater authority than belongs to them in their primary signification. And perhaps the adapted meaning surpasses the original by as much as the reality excels the image ; the light, the shadow ; the mistress, the maid-servant.

" To-day you shall know that the Lord will come." It appears to me, my brethren, that in these words we have expressly commended to our notice two days of unequal duration. The first of these embraces the whole period from the fall of the first man to the dissolution of the world. It is the day which the saints, as we read, have so often cursed. For when Adam was exiled from that most luminous day of innocence in which he had been created, and thrust out into the miseries consequent on his sin, he entered upon a day of spiritual darkness in which the light of truth was all but extinguished. We have been born, every one of us, in this darksome day, if day it may be called and not rather night. However, I will call it day on account of the light of reason, which, as a glimmering spark, has been left to relieve its gloom,

by God's unconquerable mercy.* But the second day
shall shine " in the splendours of the saints " for everlasting ages, after the break of that most serene
morning (whereon we hope and pray that mercy
shall be granted us) when death shall be " swallowed up in victory," and when the brightness of
the true and living Light shall occupy all things
above and below, within and without, expelling
the shadows and the darkness.   " Cause me to
hear Thy mercy in the morning," implores the
Psalmist, and elsewhere he acknowledges, " We are
filled in the morning with Thy mercy."   But let us
return to our own day, which by reason of its com-
parative brevity is called " a watch of the night,"
which is " counted as nothing and vanity " by that
familiar mouthpiece of the Holy Ghost who says,
" all our days have vanished," and, " my days are
vanished like smoke," and, " my days have declined
like a shadow." The holy Patriarch Jacob, who
" saw the Lord face to face " and conversed with Him
so familiarly, spoke of the days of his pilgrimage as
" few and evil." Nevertheless, even in this day
God gives man the light of reason and understanding.
But it is further necessary that, at the moment of
our departure from this world, He shall illumine our
souls with the splendour of His own divine knowledge.

* " For the first man, Adam, being corrupted by sin, the
punishment of his sin has descended upon all mankind.   So
that nature itself, which by Thee was created good and right,
is now put for the vice and infirmity of corrupt nature ; because
the motion thereof, left to itself, draws to evil and to things
below.   For the little strength which remains is but like a
spark hidden in the ashes.   This is our natural reason, which
is surrounded with a great mist, having yet the judgment of
good and evil, and of the distance of truth and falsehood "
(*Imitation of Christ* Bk. III. ch. lv.).

For were we to go forth in darkness out of the prison-house of the body and from the shadow of death, our darkness could never more be enlightened. Here is the reason why the only-begotten Son of God, the Sun of justice, has shown Himself amidst the gloom of this place of our banishment as a burning and shining Torch, of large and brilliant flame, in order, namely, that all who desire to be illuminated may approach and be united to Him so closely as to leave nothing intervening between Him and them. For it is our sins that " separate between us and God." Therefore, as soon as these are removed, we are placed in contact with the true Light of the world, to be enlightened by and, as it were, made one with It ; just as when we want to light an extinguished taper we touch it to another that is burning and shining, if I may be allowed to illustrate an invisible truth by an example drawn from things visible.

Let us, therefore, my brethren, light for ourselves the lamp of knowledge—as the Prophet speaks *—at this great and luminous Star, before we pass out of the darkness of this world. Otherwise we shall only exchange darkness for denser darkness, the darkness of time for the darkness of eternity. But what is this knowledge which is so necessary for us to possess ? It is to know that the Lord will come, even though we cannot ascertain the time of His coming. This, my brethren, is the sum-total of the knowledge required of us. But I may be told that so much knowledge is in the possession of all. " For who," it will be said, " even amongst nominal Christians, is not aware that the

* Osee x. 12 (according to the Septuagint Version).—Translator.)

Lord will come,—' that He will come again to judge the living and the dead,' and to ' render to every man according to his works ? ' " I answer by denying that all have this knowledge, or even many. It belongs but to the few, because in truth, it is only the few that shall be saved.* Do you suppose that they " who are glad when they have done evil and rejoice in most wicked things," do you suppose that such persons have the knowledge and the remembrance of the Lord's future coming ? Should they tell you so, believe them not, because, as St. John Evangelist bears witness, " He who saith that he knoweth Him and keepeth not His commandments, is a liar." And, according to St. Paul, " They profess that they know God, but in their works they deny Him." For " faith without works is dead." Surely if they had a true knowledge and fear of the coming of the Lord they would not defile their souls with all manner of moral filthiness, but would rather keep careful watch and not suffer such violence to be done to their consciences.

Now, the first degree of this knowledge produces penitence and sorrow, changing laughter into tears, song into mourning, joy into grief; insomuch that you begin to have a dislike now for what particularly pleased you before, and what you were wont to seek with the greatest avidity you avoid now with the greatest disgust. For so it is written, " He that addeth knowledge, addeth also sorrow." Hence true and holy knowledge proves its presence by the sorrow it excites. In its second degree, this knowledge produces amendment of life, so that you no longer

* See the Saint's Sermons on the Canticle of Canticles, vol. ii. 261-2.—(Translator.)

" yield your members to serve uncleanness and iniquity
unto iniquity," but instead you begin to bridle
gluttony, to mortify the passion for pleasure, to
humble your pride, and to compel your body, which
has hitherto been the instrument of sin, to co-operate
henceforth unto your sanctification. For repentance
without amendment will profit you nothing. Hence
the Wise Man says, " When one buildeth up and
another pulleth down, what profit have they but the
labour ? When one prayeth and another curseth,
whose voice will God hear ?   He that washeth himself after touching the dead, if he toucheth him again,
what doth his washing avail ? "   Rather he ought to
fear " lest some worse thing should happen to " him,
as the Saviour gives warning. But because this amendment of life cannot long be sustained, unless the soul
keeps watch and ward over herself, with wakeful and
unwearying circumscription, she has need of the third
degree of knowledge which produces solicitude, so that
she may begin to walk carefully with her God, ever
and in all things anxiously vigilant, lest she should
offend, even in the very least, the eyes of so tremendous
a Majesty.   Thus, in repentance she is warmed; in
amendment she is set on fire ; in solicitude she becomes
all luminous and radiant, so that the whole man is
renewed within and without.

The soul that attains to this third degree begins at
last to enjoy a respite from " the trouble of evils and
sorrow," and to temper with spiritual gladness the
excess of her fear, lest at the thought of the greatness
of her sins, she should " be swallowed up with over-
much sorrow."   Therefore, although she is afraid of
the Judge, she has hope in the Saviour. Fear and

joy are now contending and battling for the government of her mind. Nor seldom fear comes off
triumphant, but more often the victory rests with
joy, which puts fear to rout and shuts it up within
its own secret stronghold. Happy the conscience
wherein this conflict is being perpetually carried on
until " that which is mortal is swallowed up by life,"
until " that which is perfect"—namely, joy—reigns alone
and " that which is in part, viz., fear—shall be done
away." For it is not fear that shall endure for ever, but
only joy. Nevertheless, although such a soul is now burning and shining, let her not imagine herself to be at home
in the shelter of her own house, where a lighted torch
may be carried about without any fear of draughts.
Let her remember that she is still out under the open
sky, consequently, that she must be careful to protect
with her two hands the flame of her candle, and not to
trust it to the air, even when it appears most tranquil.
For on a sudden, and at a moment when she is not
suspecting, it will change its mood : then, if the shelter-
ing hand has been withdrawn, although but for an
instant, the light shall be promptly extinguished.
And even if (as sometimes happens) the light of the
candle begins to burn the hand that protects it, let
her rather choose to suffer the pain than to withdraw
the shelter, for otherwise, " in a moment, in the
twinkling of an eye," the flame shall be blown out.
Were we at home, in that " house not made with hands,
eternal in heaven," to which no enemy gains admission,
and from which no friend departs, then, my brethren,
we should have nothing to fear. But so long as we
live here below, we are exposed to three winds of the
greatest power and malignity, namely : the world, the

flesh, and the devil, which endeavour to extinguish the light of our conscience by blowing in upon our hearts evil desires and illicit motions, and suddenly bewildering us in such a manner that one can scarcely tell " whence he cometh or whither he goeth." Two of these spiritual winds sometimes cease from troubling us, but the third never makes a truce with anyone. Consequently, we must employ both our hands, and the hands of our souls rather than those of our body, to protect our consciences, lest perchance the light which has been kindled in them should be lost. We must not yield, we must not give way, even though the violent heat of temptation is furiously burning us in both our spiritual and material parts. But we must say with the Psalmist, " My soul is continually in my hands." Let us endure the fire rather than surrender. And as we do not easily forget what we hold in our hands, so we should never lose sight of the interests of our souls, and our spiritual concerns ought to hold the first place in our hearts.

When, therefore, our loins have been thus girded and our lamps thus lighted, we must begin to keep the " night-watches " over the flocks of our thoughts and actions, so that if the Lord shall come at the first watch, or at the second watch, or at the third, He shall always find us ready. The first of these night-watches, my brethren, is regularity in your exterior conduct, so that you endeavour to conform your whole life to the Rule you have sworn to observe, and do not transgress the bounds which our fathers have set in all the exercises of this way and life, declining neither to the right hand nor to the left. The second is purity of intention, so that the eye being simple may render the whole body lightsome. Thus, all that you do now is done purely for the glory of God, and " unto the place from whence the rivers (of grace) come they return to flow again." The third night-watch is zeal for the preservation of concord and unity. And thou keepest this when, placed in the community, thou givest the will of each of thy brethren the preference over thine own,* so that thou conversest amongst them not alone without blame, but with the kindliness of charity, supporting all and praying for all, in such a manner as to deserve to have applied to thee what Onias said of the Prophet, " This is a lover of his brethren and of all the people of Israel : this is he that prayeth much for the people and for all the holy city." It is thus, my brethren, that on this day the advent of the Only-Begotten enkindles for us the light of true knowledge : I mean the knowledge by which we know that the Lord will come, which is, the firm and enduring foundation of our spiritual life.

" And in the morning you shall see the glory of the Lord." O most desirable morning ! O day in the courts of the Lord that is " better above thousands," wherein for ever month shall succeed to month and sabbath to sabbath, whilst the splendour of light and the fervour of charity shall unfold and illumine the loftiest mysteries of God for the contemplation of the blessed ! Oh, who shall presume—I do not say, to describe—but even to imagine thy glories ? Yet, in the meantime, my brethren, let us strengthen our faith, in order that, if we cannot behold the wonders which are reserved for the life to come, we may at

* " The brethren shall obey not only the abbot, but also one another ; for it is by this way they are to reach the kingdom of heaven " (Holy Rule of St. Benedict, ch. lxxi.).

least contemplate something of the marvels accomplished
for us on earth. In assuming our flesh the Majesty
of God by an exercise of omnipotence wrought three
works, effected three unions, so uniquely wonderful
and so wonderfully unique, that nothing like them
has ever yet been done upon the earth or shall be
done hereafter. For the Divine Nature was united
to the human, virginity to motherhood, and faith to
the heart of man. Very admirable in truth is each of
these unions, and more marvellous than any miracle :
how elements so heterogeneous and, in a sense, so
opposed, could be brought together and made to
combine.

And consider first of all the creation of the universe,
and the disposition and ordering of its various parts.
What a display of power in the production of a world
out of nothingness ! What wisdom in the collocation
of the different orders of creatures ! What benignity in
their manifold combination ! Reflect on the multitude
and magnitude of the things created by almighty power,
how wisely they are all distributed, with how much
goodness they have been compounded, the highest being
united to the lowest, with a charity as amiable as it
is admirable. For to this slime of the earth has been
added the vital force, as for instance, in the trees
where its presence is manifested in the beauty of the
foliage, in the brilliancy of the flowers, and in the
sweetness and wholesomeness of the fruit. Not content
with thus ennobling our common clay, the Creator
has further endowed it with the principle of sentiency
in the brute beasts, which are not only gifted with
life but also possess a fivefold faculty of perception.
And He has stopped not even at this, but in order to

honour the material element still more, He has
associated with it the rational soul in the case of
man, who, in addition to life and sensibility, is invested with the power of discriminating between
what is helpful and what is harmful, between good
and evil, between truth and falsity. Lastly, the Divine
Majesty, wishing to elevate matter to a yet higher
glory, contracted His own immensity and gave Himself—the greatest gift in His power to bestow—to be
united to our earthy substance, so that in the unity of
a single Person should be wedded together God and
matter, Majesty and weakness, infinite Sublimity and
utter abjection. For there is nothing more sublime
than the Divinity and nothing more abject than clay.
And nevertheless with so much condescension has God
lowered Himself to the level of matter, with so much
honour has matter been raised to the level of God,
that by an ineffable and incomprehensible mystery,
whatever God has done in it, matter may be said to
have done, and whatever matter has suffered in Him,
God may be said to have suffered. * But observe here

* This is the doctrine of the " communication of idioms,"
according to which it is lawful to attribute to Christ as man
what belongs to Him only as He is God, and *vice versa*. Thus
we may say that the Second Person of the Blessed Trinity was
crucified, that the Author of life was slain, that Mary's Son
created the world, etc. St. Thomas gives the reason (*Sum.
Theol.*, III. q. xvi. a. 4), " Et hujus ratio est quia cum sit eadem
hypostasis utriusque naturae, eadem hypostasis supponitur
nomine utriusque naturae. Sive ergo dicatur (Christus) homo
sive Deus, supponitur hypostasis divinae et humanae naturae.
Et ideo de homine dici possunt ea quae sunt divinae naturae
tanquam de hypostasi divinae naturae ; et de Deo possunt dici
ea quae sunt humanae naturae, tanquam de hypostasi humanae
naturae." But in the next article he reminds us that this is not
possible when we employ abstract substantives, which do not
signify the Person : we may not say, for example, that the
Divinity suffered or that the *Humanity* of Christ created the

that, just as in the Godhead there is unity of Substance with trinity of Persons, so, in this special composition, we have a trinity of substances, with a unity of Person. And as in the former case, neither the plurality of Persons prejudices the unity of Substance, nor does the unity of Substance exclude the distinction of the Persons ; so likewise in the latter, neither the unity of the Person confounds the distinction of the substances, nor does the plurality of the substances destroy the unity of the Person. My brethren, the Divine and Sovereign Trinity has exhibited to us this inferior trinity as the most wonderful thing in creation, as a work singular amongst all and over all the multitudinous works of God. For here the Word, the soul, and human flesh are united in the unity of a single Person. These three are One, and this One is three, not by any confusion of the substances, but by the unity of the Person of the Word. This is the first and most excellent union, it is the first amongst the three unions to which I have referred. Remember, O man, that thou art but dust, and be not proud ; remember also that thou art made one with God and be not ungrateful.

The second union is the truly singular and admirable alliance of virginity with motherhood. " From the beginning of the world it hath not been heard " that one who brought forth remained still a virgin, or that one who remained a virgin brought forth. According to the ordinary course of nature, virginity is never found co-existent with fecundity, nor is there any room for fecundity where virginity is preserved intact. Mary

world, because such terms express only the nature, whereas it is true to say that God suffered and died, and that the Man Christ created the world. Cf. Hurter, vol. ii. p. 423.—(Translator.)

is the only woman in whom integrity and motherhood
have met together.   In her was once accomplished
what had never been done before nor shall be done
hereafter, for it is of her the Poet sings,

" Whose like had ne'er been seen before,
Nor shall appear for evermore."—(Sedulius).

The third union is that of faith with the human
heart. This, although inferior in dignity, both to the
first and to the second, is yet perhaps their equal in
strength. For it is very extraordinary, how the heart
of man yields the assent of faith to those two mysteries,
how it can believe that God has become man, and
that Mary has remained a virgin after child-birth.
Just as iron and clay cannot be welded together, so
it is equally impossible to conjoin so mighty a force
of faith with the weakness and inconstancy of the
human heart, without the solder of the Holy Spirit.
Are we then to believe that He Who is laid in the
manger, Who weeps in the cradle, Who suffers all the
miseries and pains incidental to childhood, Who is
scourged, Who is spat upon, Who is crucified, Who
is placed in the sepulchre and confined between two
stones—are we to believe Him to be God, God
immense and majestic ?   And' with regard to Mary,
how can we believe in the virginity of her whom
we behold suckling her Babe, who lives with her
husband and is always at his side, accompanying
him in his long journey to Egypt and back again to
Nazareth ?   How can the human race, how can the
whole world be induced to credit this ?   Nevertheless,
these truths have won acceptance, and that with so
much power and facility that the very multitude of

those who believe in them makes them credible to me. Yea, " young men and maidens, the old with the younger," have chosen to die a thousand deaths rather than renounce this faith for a moment.

This third union is indeed very excellent, but still more excellent is the second, and most excellent of all is the first. " Ear hath heard " of the first, although " eye hath not seen " it. For that " great mystery of godliness " has been heard and believed even to the ends of the earth. But " eye hath not seen, O God, besides Thee," how Thou hast united Thyself to a human body within the narrow limits of a virgin's womb. " Eye hath seen " the second union, because that glorious Queen who " kept all these words pondering them in her heart," saw herself at one and the same time a mother and a virgin. And Joseph also was no less the witness than the guardian of his consort's integrity. The third " hath entered into the heart of man," when what was accomplished was believed as it had been accomplished, when more credit was given to the oracle of heaven than to the human eye, when men believed firmly, nothing doubting, the things that were said or done. Therefore, in the first of these three unions, thou mayest perceive what God has bestowed upon thee, in the second by what intermediary He has bestowed it, and in the third for what purpose. He has given thee Christ, through Mary, for thy salvation. Hence the first union contains the remedy : it is a poultice, so to speak, made up of the Divine Nature and the human, and intended for the cure of thy infirmities. These two elements have been ground and mixed in the mortar of the Virgin's bosom; the Holy Spirit, as the pestle, sweetly blending them

together.   But since thou wert unworthy to receive so
great a gift directly from the Lord, it was given to Mary,
so that thou mightest receive through her hands whatever of good was destined for thee—through her hands, I
say, who by her motherhood has for thee given birth to
God, and because she was a virgin has been " heard for
(her) reverence," when pleading thy cause and the cause
of the whole human race.   Were she a mother alone,
it would be enough for her to " be saved through child-
bearing," as the Apostle speaks; and were she a virgin
alone, she would be sufficient for herself indeed, but
there would be no fruit of her womb to be pronounced
blessed, or to become the world's ransom.   Therefore,
whilst the first union contains the remedy, it is only
in the second that we enjoy the benefit of that remedy,
because it is the will of God that we should have
nothing which has not passed through the hands of
Mary.   In the third of these unions we find merit,
for it is accounted merit to us when we believe firmly
in the two preceding; and there is salvation in faith,
as the Lord assures us, where He says, " He that
believeth shall be saved."   Amen.

FOURTH SERMON FOR CHRISTMAS EVE

ON THE SPIRITUAL RICHES WHICH CHRIST BROUGHT ON EARTH

" Length of days is in (His) right hand and in (His) left hand riches and glory."—Prov. iii. 16.

The custom of our Order, my brethren, does not require that there should be a sermon to-day. But considering that on to-morrow we shall be occupied so long in the celebration of Masses that the time left over will be too short for a discourse of the usual length, I have thought it advisable to prepare your hearts now for so great a solemnity; especially because this mystery is so unfathomably profound, so absolutely incomprehensible, that like a never-failing fountain, it can be exhausted by no prodigality, but the more it communicates, the more it has to give. I know well, my dear children, how great is the tribulation you are enduring for the love of Christ, and I pray God that your consolation in Him may be equally abundant. As for earthly comforts, I have neither the wish nor the right to offer you anything of that sort. Such consolation is vile, and can serve no useful purpose; and what is more to be feared, it is often a hindrance to true and salutary consolation. And so, in order that we may possess this desirable consolation and repudiate the false, He Who is the everlasting crown and delight of the angels has become Himself the salvation and consolation of the miserable; He, Who as a mighty and noble Monarch fills His subjects with happiness in His kingdom beyond the stars, greatly rejoices us poor exiles in the place of our banishment by appearing amongst us as little and lowly; He Who is the "Glory of God in the highest" is made "on earth Peace to men of good will." For He is given as a Little One to them who are themselves little, so that being made great by Him, they may receive Him as great, and that whom He justifies now in His littleness, He may afterwards in His Majesty and magnificence exalt and glorify. Hence, no doubt, the Vessel of Election "hath uttered the good word" which he received from the fulness of this Little One—for although little, He is nevertheless full, "full of grace and truth," since "in Him dwelleth all the fulness of the Godhead corporally"—hence it is, I say, that St. Paul "hath uttered the good word" which you have frequently heard during these days: "Rejoice in the Lord always, again I say, rejoice." That is, he bids you to rejoice firstly on account of the grace which is given you, and to rejoice secondly on account of the glory which is promised, because both the gift and the hope are alike full of gladness: he bids you to rejoice over the largess which you have received from the Left Hand and to rejoice over the reward which you expect from the Right. For the Spouse in the Canticle says, speaking of the Bridegroom, "His Left Hand is under my head, and His Right shall embrace me." With His Left Hand He supports us,but with His Right He draws us to Himself; with His Left He cures and pardons, but with the Right He caresses and glorifies; His Left Hand holds merit, but in His Right is contained the reward; in His "Right Hand are delights

even to the end," but in His Left are found health
and healing.

But observe the loving-kindness, observe the wisdom
of this Divine Physician of our souls. Consider carefully
how novel are the remedies He brings. Notice that
His medicines are not only precious but also beautiful,
not alone most useful for restoring to us our health,
but at the same time pleasing to the eye and sweet
to the palate. Look at His first remedy, the
first gift which He bears in His Left Hand. You
shall find it to be His virginal conception. Reflect, I
pray you, on the nature of this. How strange it is,
how admirable, how amiable, how delightful! For
what can be more beautiful than " a chaste generation " ? What more glorious than a pure and holy
conception, free from all stain, from all shame, from
all corruption ? But because the grandeur of this
unique conception, admirable as it is, would not,
nevertheless, have been likely to interest me so
much if its attractions were not reinforced by the
hope of salvation and the consideration of my own
utility, therefore was it (the conception) not only
made magnificent in its outward show, but also
rendered precious in its inward virtue, thus verifying
what is written in the Proverbs, " In (His) Left Hand
are riches and glory," that is to say, the riches of
salvation and the glory of novelty. For " who can
make him clean that is conceived of unclean seed "
but He alone Whose conception alone was free
from the influence of carnal concupiscence? We, my
brethren, have all of us been defiled and infected in
our very root and origin : our conception has been
sullied. But there is One Who can take away our

shame, He, namely, upon Whom alone this shame
has never fallen.

I have, therefore, the riches of salvation, I have
the most pure conception of Christ, wherewith I may
redeem the impurity of my own. But continue, O
Lord Jesus, continue to add new marvels to the old,
and to work ever fresh wonders, because the prodigies
already wrought have lost, through familiarity, their
power to impress us. Miracles undoubtedly, and great
miracles, are the rising and the setting of the sun, the
fertility of the earth, the succession of the seasons,
etc., but they are so constantly before our eyes that
they attract no attention.* Therefore, O Lord, renew
Thy signs and change Thy prodigies. " Behold," He
says, " I make all things new." Who speaks thus ?
It is the Lamb " That sitteth on the throne," the Lamb
of God, all sweetness, all delight, all unction. I say
" all unction," for this is the meaning of the name
He bears, Christ being the Greek for " anointed."
What indeed can there be of harshness or austerity
in Him Who even in His nativity, inflicted on His
Mother neither pain nor loss ? O truly unprecedented

---

* St. Augustine repeatedly expresses the same thought.
Thus (quaest. lxxix.) he says, " Although the miracles which
occur in the ordinary course of visible nature are so common
and familiar that they attract no attention, yet if one reflects
he will recognise that they are really greater than those which
happen rarely " ; and again (in Joan. 24), " The government
of the universe is a greater miracle than the feeding of five
thousand men with five loaves ; and if the latter appears more
wonderful, it is not because it is a mightier manifestation of
of power and wisdom, but only because it is more rare."
However, such natural processes and phenomena would not
be called miracles in the technical sense. For a miracle in
this sense the Scholastics require that the fact be " sensible,
supernatural, rare, and wrought by divine power." Cf. Hickey,
Summula. Phil. Schol., v. ii. p. 181.—(Translator.)

marvels ! A Child is conceived without shame and brought forth without sorrow ! The curse pronounced upon Eve, is for our Virgin changed into a blessing ! For neither pain nor sorrow attended Mary's childbirth. The malediction, I say, has become a benediction, so that now, O happy Mother, as was predicted of thee by Gabriel, " Blessed art thou among women." O happy Virgin, happy in that, alone of all women, thou hast escaped the curse and obtained the blessing ; in that thou alone has been delivered from the universal malediction, and freed from the sorrows of mother-hood ! Nor should it surprise us, my brethren, that *He* at His birth caused His Mother no sorrow, Who came, according to the prediction of the Prophet Isaias, to take away the sorrows of the whole world, because, in truth, " He hath borne our infirmities and carried our sorrows." There are two things especially which our human fragility is afraid of, and these are suffering and disgrace. Christ came to deliver us from them both and therefore took them both upon Himself when—to pass over His other afflictions and humiliations—He was condemned to die by the im-pious, and to die a death of shame. Hence, in order to give us an assurance of His purpose to save us from suffering and ignominy, He began by making His own Mother immune from both, for she conceived without confusion and brought forth without pain.

But the riches of salvation are made still more abounding, the glory increases, fresh wonders are witnessed, new miracles are wrought. Not only is the Child conceived without shame and brought forth without sorrow, but the Mother, too, has preserved her virginity intact. O prodigy unheard of ! A Virgin

brings forth and after parturition remains a virgin
inviolate ; combining maternal fecundity with virginal
integrity,

" In whom
The mother's joy enhanced the virgin's bloom." *

Now I can expect with confidence the glory of incorruption promised to my own flesh by Christ when
I behold Him preserving incorruption in the flesh of
His Mother. For it will not be hard to Him Who
caused His Mother to bring forth without prejudice
to her virginity, to cause " this corruptible body " to
" put on incorruption " in a glorious resurrection.

But the Left Hand holds riches still more
abundant and glories still more sublime. Mary is
made a mother without losing her virginity and her
Child is conceived and born free from every stain of
sin. The Mother is preserved from the curse pronounced upon Eve ; the Child is immune from that
universal condition whereof holy Job has declared,
" No one is free from stain, not even the infant who
has lived one day upon the earth." Yet behold here
an Infant without spot or stain, Who is alone true
amongst men, yea, Who is Truth Itself. Behold
" the Lamb without blemish," " behold the Lamb of
God, behold Him Who taketh away the sin of the
world." For who is better able to destroy our sins than
He on Whom sin has never fallen ? He Who has
never, as I know, been defiled Himself, has doubtless
the power to cleanse me from my stains. Let that
Hand which alone is clean wipe away the mud which

---

* " Quae ventre beato
 Gaudio matris habens cum virginitatis honore."
Sedulius, Carm. Pasch. ii. 37-38.

covers my eyes. Let Him "cast the mote out of (my) eye" Who has no beam in His own. I should rather have said, let Him remove the beam from my eye Whose own eye is dimmed by no smallest speck of dust.*

Certainly, we have now seen the riches of salvation and life : "we have seen His glory, the glory as it were of the Only-Begotten of the Father." Of what Father, do you inquire ? Listen to the Angel : "And He shall be called the Son of the Most High." There is no need to explain who the Most High is. But to leave no room for even an unreasonable doubt, the heavenly envoy continues, speaking to the Virgin, " and therefore also the Holy which shall be born of thee shall be called the Son of God." Oh, how truly is He called the Holy ! Lord, " Thou wilt not give Thy Holy One to see corruption," for He has not permitted His Mother " to see corruption." Miracles are multiplied, riches more abound, treasures are revealed. She who brings forth is a virgin and a mother, He Who is brought forth is God and man. But shall that which is holy be given to dogs ? Shall pearls be cast before swine ? Surely no. Therefore let our treasure be hidden in the field, let our money be placed in the coffer. Let the virginal conception be concealed under the mantle of the Mother's espousals ; let the painless child-birth be veiled behind the Infant's cries and sufferings. Let the legal purification hide the Mother's integrity, and the common circumcision the innocence of the Child. Conceal, O Virgin, conceal, I pray thee, the brightness of this new Sun. Place the

* Cf. Luke vi. 41-42 ; John ix. 6-7.

Infant in the manger, wrap Him in the swaddling clothes. These swaddling clothes are themselves also a part of our riches. The Saviour's swaddling clothes are to us more precious than any purple. The manger wherein He reposes is in our eyes more glorious than the gilded seats of monarchs. Rich beyond all riches and treasures is the poverty of Christ. For what can be richer, what can be found more precious than Christian humility, wherewith the kingdom of heaven may be purchased and the grace of God acquired? Hence it is written, " Blessed are the poor in spirit, for theirs is the kingdom of heaven," and the Apostle St. James tells us that " God resisteth the proud and giveth His grace to the humble." But here in the nativity we have the virtue of humility commended to us by the example of God Himself. For it was in humility that " He emptied Himself, taking the form of a servant, being made in the likeness of men and in habit found as a man."

Do you wish, my brethren, to find riches still more precious, and a glory more excellent still? Then consider the charity of Christ as revealed in His passion. As He declares Himself, " Greater love than this no man hath, that a man lay down his life for his friends." Here indeed are our riches and our glory, the Precious Blood by Which we have been redeemed, and the cross of the Lord wherein we glory with St. Paul, saying like him, " God forbid that I should glory save in the cross of the Lord Jesus Christ." It was the same Apostle who said, " I judged not myself to know any-thing among you but Jesus Christ and Him crucified." This is the Left Hand of God, namely, " Jesus Christ and the Same crucified." The Right Hand is Jesus

Christ and the Same glorified. " Jesus Christ," says the great Apostle, "and Him crucified." Perhaps, my brethren, we ourselves are this cross on which Christ is affirmed to be crucified. For the very figure of our body represents the cross, as will more evidently appear if you extend your arms. In one of the psalms Christ says of Himself, " I am fixed in the slime of the deep." Now it is manifest that we are slime, because from the slime of the earth we were fashioned. Originally, as you know, we were the slime of paradise, but now we are the slime of the deep. " I am fixed," says the Saviour, " I have not passed over, I have not gone back. I am with you all days even to the consummation of the world." For He is Emmanuel, that is to say, " God with us." He abides with us on earth, but by His Left Hand. Thus of old, when Thamar was about to be delivered of twins, Zara first put forth a single hand, which the midwife tied with a scarlet thread to symbolise the mystery of the Lord's passion.*

Therefore we hold the Left Hand already. But it is still necessary for us to cry with Job, " To the work of Thy Hands reach out Thy Right Hand," because " in Thy Right Hand are delights even to the end." O Lord, extend Thy Right Hand " and it is enough for us." " Glory and wealth," sings the Psalmist, " shall be in his house," that is, in the house of him who fears the Lord. But what, O Lord, shall be in Thine own house ? Thanksgiving, surely, and the voice of praise. For so the Royal Prophet says, " Blessed are they that dwell in Thy house, O Lord ; they shall praise Thee for ever and ever." And according to the

* Cf. Genesis xxxviii. 27-30.

Apostle, " Eye hath not seen, nor ear heard, neither hath it ascended (ascendit) into the heart of man what things God hath prepared for them that love Him." These things, my brethren, are the " light inaccessible," and the " peace that surpasseth all understanding," and the fountain whose waters love to descend and never rise above their source. For " eye hath not seen " the " light inaccessible," " nor ear heard " that peace incomprehensible. " How beautiful are the feet of them that preach the Gospel of peace ! " But although " their sound hath gone forth into all the earth," yet how great is that " peace which surpasseth all understanding " the preachers themselves are unable to comprehend, not to speak of conveying it to the minds of their hearers. For attend to the words of St. Paul : " Brethren," he says, " I do not count myself to have apprehended." And he tells us in another place that " faith cometh by hearing and hearing by the word of Christ." But faith is not sight, nor is the promise of peace the bestowal thereof. True, even now there is " peace on earth to men of good will." Yet what is that peace compared to the fulness and excellence of the peace which awaits us in heaven ? Hence the Lord says, speaking to His apostles, " Peace I leave with you, My peace I give unto you," which may be paraphrased thus : " You are not as yet capable of receiving My peace which surpasseth all understanding, and is a peace above peace. Therefore I give you now in promise the kingdom of peace, and leave you in the meanwhile the way of peace."

But what means the expression, " neither hath it *ascended* into the heart of man " ? The Apostle doubtless designs to teach us by these words that the peace of heaven resembles the stream of a fountain which knows not how to ascend. For you are not ignorant that it is the nature of flowing water to follow the slope of the valleys and to pour itself down from the mountain heights. Hence it is written, " Thou sendest forth springs in the vales, between the midst of the hills the waters shall pass." This is the reason, my brethren, why I am so often solicitous to remind your charity that " God resisteth the proud and giveth grace to the humble." For the waters of a fountain never rise above the level of their source.* But according to this rule it may appear to you that pride can be no obstacle to the currents of grace, especially because that first proud creature who, according to holy Job, " is king over all the children of pride," is not represented to have said, " I will be *higher* than the Most High," but " I will be like the Most High." Nevertheless the Apostle does not lie when he affirms of Satan that he " is lifted up above all that is called God or that is worshipped." The human ear is horrified at such blasphemous language. But would to God the wicked thought and feeling it expresses were equally an object of horror to the human heart ! For I say to you that not Lucifer alone but every other proud being as well, " is lifted above all that is called God or worshipped." And I will prove this. The Creator requires that His will shall be done, and the proud

* Here, as often elsewhere, the Saint leaves the application of the metaphor to the intelligence of his hearers. What he is insinuating in this passage is obvious enough : the stream of grace cannot rise above its source, and since it has its source in the humble Heart of Jesus, therefore it cannot be communicated to the proud and high-minded.—(Translator.)

creature wants his own will done. So far there is the appearance of equality. But observe now how great is the difference. For God wants His will to be done only in those things which reason approves, whereas the proud creature insists on having his way with or without reason. You perceive how he thus makes a mountain of himself up the steepness of which the waters of grace cannot flow. Hence the Saviour tells us, " Unless you be converted and become as little children, you shall not enter into the kingdom of heaven. Whosoever therefore shall humble himself as this little child,* he is the greater in the kingdom of heaven." The little Child He presents to us as our Model is none other than Himself, Who is the Well-Spring of life, in Whom dwells and from Whom proceeds the fulness of all graces. Therefore make ready the channels in which grace may flow, level down the heights of proud and earthly thoughts, conform yourselves to the Son of man, not to the first father of men, because the stream of grace ascendeth not into the heart of man, that is to say, into the uplifted heart of the carnal and earthly minded. Cleanse your eyes also, that you may be able to gaze upon that light of infinite purity, and incline your ears to obedience, that you may sometime attain to that everlasting repose and to that peace above all peace. The happiness of heaven is called light because of its purity, peace because of its tranquillity, a fountain because of its eternity and abundance. We may

---

* There is a tradition that this child was St. Martial, who later became a disciple of St. Peter and preached the Gospel in Gaul. Another account identifies him with St. Ignatius, the illustrious Bishop of Antioch, martyred in the year 107. St. Bernard's interpretation is purely accommodative. Cf. A Lapide, *Comment. in Matth.* xviii. 2.—(Translator.)

assign the fountain to the Father, from Whom the
Son is born and the Holy Ghost proceeds ; the light
to the Son, Who is in truth " the Brightness of Eternal
Light " and " the true Light Which enlighteneth every
man that cometh into this world " ; and the peace to
the Holy Ghost, Who is said to rest upon the humble
and the quiet.   But I must not be understood to imply
that these attributes are so proper to the individual
Persons as not to belong equally to all.   For the Father
also is Light since the Son is " Light of Light " ; and
the Son also is Peace, because, as the Apostle tells us,
He is " our Peace Who hath made both one " ; and
the Holy Spirit also is a " Fountain of water springing
up unto life everlasting."

But when shall we attain to this Light, to this
Peace, to this Fountain ?   When, O Lord, wilt Thou
" fill me with joy with Thy Countenance " ?   We
rejoice in Thee now since Thou, " the Orient from on
high, hath visited us."   We rejoice also " looking for
the blessed hope " of Thy second coming.   But when
shall we be given the fulness of joy, not in promise,
but in fact ?   When shall we rejoice not in the hope
but in the possession of that plenitude ?   " Let your
modesty be known to all men," says the Apostle,
" the Lord is nigh."   It is indeed only right that our
modesty should become known, just as the modesty
of the Lord our God has been made manifest to all.
For what could be more incongruous than that men
should behave with arrogance, though conscious of
their own infirmity, and after beholding the Lord
of Majesty living a modest life amongst them ?
" Learn of Me," He says, " because I am meek and
humble of heart, and thus *your* modesty also shall

become known to all men." But as regards the words which follow in the passage from St. Paul, namely, " The Lord is nigh," it is necessary to understand them of the Right Hand. For with reference to the Left Hand the Lord Himself has said, " Behold I am with you all days even to the consummation of the world." " The Lord is nigh," my brethren. Therefore " be nothing solicitous." He is already at hand and will presently appear. Do not lose courage, do not grow weary. " Seek ye the Lord while He may be found ; call upon Him while He is near." " The Lord is nigh unto them that are of a contrite heart " ; " the Lord is nigh unto all them that call upon Him, to all that call upon Him in truth." And do you wish to know how near He is ? Then listen to the Spouse in the Canticle where she sings of her Beloved : " Behold He standeth behind our wall." By this wall we are to understand our mortal body which intervenes as an obstacle during the present life, and hinders us from seeing Him Who standeth behind.* Therefore the Apostle desired to be dissolved and to be with Christ, exclaiming in his wretchedness, " Unhappy man that I am, who shall deliver me from the body of this death ? " And the Psalmist gives expression to the same desire where he sings, " Bring my soul out of prison that I may praise Thy name."

* Cf. Sermon LVI on the Canticle of Canticles.—(Translator.)

FIFTH SERMON FOR CHRISTMAS EVE

On the Manner in which we must prepare and sanctify ourselves for the Vision of God

" Sanctify yourselves to-day and be ye prepared, for to-morrow you shall see in you the Majesty of God."—From the Responsory of the Office of Vigils for Christmas Eve.

To-day, my brethren, on the eve of the Lord's nativity, the Church wisely admonishes us to prepare ourselves in all holiness for the celebration of so unspeakable a mystery. For the Holy of Holies is at hand : He is at hand Who has said, " Be ye holy, because I the Lord your God am holy." How can that which is holy be given to dogs, or how can pearls be offered to swine, unless the dogs are first converted from their wickedness and the swine cleansed from their foulness, and unless they are resolved for the future to shun with all solicitude, the former the vomit, the latter the slough ? Of old, when the carnal Israelites were about to receive the commandments of God, they sanctified themselves with the justifications of the flesh, with various ablutions, with gifts and sacrifices, none of which things had the power of purifying the conscience of him who performed them. But now all these rites and ceremonies have passed away, because they were only given to be observed until the time of interior justification by the grace of redemption, which time, as you know, has already come. Rightly therefore has perfect holiness been from that moment expected and demanded of us, rightly has purification of the conscience been enjoined and spiritual cleanliness exacted. For the Lord Himself has said, " Blessed are the clean of heart, for they shall see God." For this we live, my brethren, for this we have been born, for this we have been called, for this it has been granted us to see the sun to-day. It was night in times past when no man was able to do these things. It was night all over the world before the dawn of the true Light, before the birth of the Saviour. It was also night for each one of us before his conversion to God and his spiritual regeneration.

Shall it be questioned that a most profound night and densest darkness covered the whole face of the earth, when our fathers of old worshipped gods made with hands, and with a sacrilegious madness fell down in adoration before stocks and stones? And with regard to each of ourselves, was it not gloomy night whilst we were " living without God in this world," whilst we were " going after our lusts," whilst we were consenting to our carnal inclinations, whilst we were obeying " worldly desires," whilst we were yielding our " members as instruments of iniquity unto sin," whilst we were " serving uncleanness and iniquity unto iniquity," " of which we are now ashamed " as of the works of darkness? Hence the Apostle says, " They that sleep, sleep in the night, and they that are drunk are drunk in the night." Such have we been, my brethren ; but we have been awakened and sanctified, if yet we be the sons of light and day rather than of night and of darkness. For he is the herald of day who cries out to us, " Be sober and watch." And to the Jews the same Apostle (St. Peter) said on the feast of Pentecost, speaking of his fellow-disciples, " These are not drunk as you suppose, seeing that it is but the third hour of the day." This is also the burden of his brother-apostle, St. Paul, where he says, " The night is passed and the day is as hand. Let us therefore cast off the works of darkness and put on the armour of light." " Let us cast off the works of darkness," such as drowsiness and drunkenness—since, as you have just heard, " they that sleep, sleep in the night ; and they that are drunk are drunk in the night," —and, as being now in the day, let us not slumber but " walk," and let us " walk honestly," not with the staggering steps of the wine-bibber. Do you see a man whose " soul slumbereth through heaviness " with regard to every good work ? Such a one " is in darkness even until now." Do you see a man " inebriated with wormwood," " more wise than it behoveth to be wise," and not " wise unto sobriety," whose " eye is not filled with seeing, neither is his ear filled with hearing," who, loving money or something similar, longs for it with a desire as insatiable as the thirst of a dropsical patient ? He is the son of night and darkness. These two evils of sloth and inordinate desire are not easy to separate. Hence it is said in Holy Scripture that " the idle man is full of desires " ; * that is to say every sluggard is given to intemperance. Let us therefore sanctify ourselves to-day, and let us be prepared. Let us prepare ourselves to-day by shaking off the drowsiness which belongs to the night ; and let us sanctify ourselves as in the day, and cleanse ourselves from nocturnal excesses, restraining the impetuosity of wicked desires. In other words, let us avoid

* The text most nearly resembling this in the Vulgate is Proverbs xxi. 25 : " Desires kill the slothful man."—(Translator.)

evil and do good, because " on these two commandments dependeth the whole law and the prophets."

But it is only for to-day we shall be thus employed.
To-morrow we shall spend neither in sanctifying ourselves, nor in preparing ourselves, but in contemplating
the Divine Majesty. For so sings the Church in her
office, " To-morrow you shall see in you the Majesty
of God." This is the same as what the Patriarch
Jacob said of old, " My justice shall answer for me
to-morrow." To-day we cultivate justice, to-morrow
it will respond to our labours. It is exercised to-day,
it will bear fruit to-morrow. For no man shall reap
what he has not sown. So he who now neglects internal
holiness shall not be admitted hereafter to the contemplation of Majesty ; the Sun of glory shall never
shine on him on whom the Sun of justice has not
risen ; nor shall he see the dawn of to-morrow who
has not lived in the light of to-day. For, as the
Apostle teaches, the same Christ, " Who of God is
made unto us Justice " to-day, shall appear as our
Life to-morrow, when we " also shall appear with Him
in glory." To-day He is born for us as a Little One,
" that man may no more presume to magnify himself
upon earth," but that we may rather " be converted
and become as little children." But to-morrow He
will show Himself to us as the " great Lord and
greatly to be praised," so that we also shall be magnified
in glory when " every man shall have praise from God."
For those whom He justifies to-day, He will magnify
to-morrow, and to the consummation of holiness shall
succeed the vision of Majesty. Neither is that an unprofitable vision which constitutes a resemblance to the
Godhead. For " we shall be like to Him, *because* we

shall see Him as He is." Hence in our text also it is not said simply, " you shall see the Majesty of God," but, " you shall see *in you* the Majesty of God." That is : to-day, when He appears in our human nature, we see ourselves in Him as in a mirror ; but to-morrow we shall see Him in ourselves, when He will clothe us with His own Divinity, when He will unveil to us His Countenance, when He will take us to Himself. This is the promise He has made to those who watch for His coming, " that He will gird Himself and make them sit down to meat and passing will minister to them." Meantime, we all receive of His fulness, not yet indeed glory for glory, but only " grace for grace." But it is written, " The Lord will give grace and glory." Despise not, therefore, the foregoing gifts if you wish to obtain the following. Do not disdain the food which is first served if you would partake of that which comes after. Even for the sake of the dish which contains it, refuse not the meat that is offered. For our Divine Peace-Maker has fashioned for Himself an incorruptible dish, " fitting " to Himself an incorruptible Body, and in this most precious dish He ministers to us the food of salvation. " Thou wilt not give Thy Holy One," sings the Psalmist, " to see corruption." And it is of the Same the Angel Gabriel says to Mary, " The Holy Which shall be born of thee shall be called the Son of God."

Therefore, let us be sanctified to-day by this Holy One, in order that we may see His Majesty in us when that future day shall dawn. For the day of sanctification has already shone upon us, and the day of salvation, but not yet the day of glory and of bliss. It is only proper that so long as the passion of the

Holy One (Who suffered on the Parasceve, that is, on
the day of preparation) is still announced, it should
be said to all, " Sanctify yourselves to-day and be
prepared.   Sanctify yourselves more and more, by
advancing from virtue to virtue, and prepare yourselves by perseverance in good."   But in what things
are we to be sanctified ?   I have read in the Scriptures
of Moses, how that the Lord " sanctified him in his
faith and meekness."   For it is quite as impossible to
please men without meekness as to please God without
faith.   Rightly, then, are we admonished to prepare
ourselves in these virtues whereby we shall give satis-
faction to God Whose Majesty we are destined to contemplate, and also to each other, so that we may behold that Majesty even in ourselves.   For this is the
reason why it behoveth us to " provide good things
not only in the sight of God, but also in the sight of
all men," namely, in order that we may render ourselves agreeable to our fellow-citizens and brothers-in-
arms, as well as to our King.

In the first place, therefore, we must seek after faith,
by which, as St. Peter testifies, God purifies our hearts.
For " blessed are the clean of heart because they shall
see (the Majesty of) God."   Abandon thyself, therefore,
to God, commit thyself to Him, " cast thy care upon
the Lord and He shall sustain thee."   Then mayest
thou say with confidence, " The Lord is careful for
me."   But such confidence is unknown to men who
love themselves, who are wise in their own conceit,
who " seek the things that are their own," and " make
provision for the flesh in its concupiscences," who are
deaf to the voice which calls out to them, saying,
" Cast all your care upon Him, for He hath care of

you." For to believe in one's self is not faith but
perfidy, and it is rather diffidence than confidence to
trust in one's self. He is truly faithful who neither
believes in himself nor hopes in himself, but, like the
Prophet, becomes to himself "as a broken vessel,"
so losing his life in this world that he may preserve
it eternally in the next. But it is only humility of
heart that can induce the faithful soul not to rely on
her own strength, but, abandoning herself, to rest upon
the Lord, and thus to "ascend from the desert, flowing
with delights, (because) leaning upon her Beloved."

But in order that our sanctification may be perfect,
it is also clearly incumbent on us to learn from the
Saint of saints the sweetness and kindliness which are
necessary in human society. Hence He Himself has
said, "Learn of Me, because I am meek and humble
of heart." But of him, who has thus made perfect his
sanctification; who "is sweet and mild and plenteous
in mercy," like God Himself; who is "all things to
all men," like the Apostle; who, in a manner, anoints
all his brethren with that ointment of gentleness and
meekness with which he is himself so saturated, so full,
so brimming over that he seems to diffuse it on every
side,—why should I not say of such a one that he is
"flowing with delights"? Happy the man who by
reason of this double preparation of faith and meekness
is able to say with the Psalmist, "My heart is ready,
O Lord, my heart is ready." For he has to-day his
"fruit unto sanctification" and to-morrow shall have
"the end, life everlasting," because to-morrow he shall
see the Majesty of God, in which everlasting life
consists, according to the words of Truth Itself, "This
is eternal life, that they may know Thee, the only

true God, and Jesus Christ Whom Thou hast sent."
And "the Lord, the just Judge, will render to (him)
in that day," to which no other shall succeed, the
"crown of justice." "Then shall he see and abound,
and his heart shall wonder and be enlarged." By how
much shall his heart be enlarged? By so much as
shall enable him to behold in himself the Majesty of
God. But do not imagine, my brethren, that I can
explain to you in words what that promise means.

"Sanctify yourselves to-day and be prepared." To-
morrow you shall see and shall rejoice, and "your
joy shall be full." For what capacity is so great that
the Majesty of God cannot fill it? Yea, you shall be
filled up and to overflowing when the "good measure,
and pressed down, and shaken together, and running
over, they shall give into your bosom." And so super-
abundant is this reward that it transcends "above
measure exceedingly" not only our merits but even
our desires. For God is able to accomplish what is
beyond our hope and power of understanding. There
are, my brethren, three ultimate objects of human
desire, namely, the honourable, the useful, and the
delectable. These are the goods which we all covet :
we all covet all of them, but in varying degrees, for
this has more attractions for one and that for another.
Thus some men are so given up to pleasure that they
have but little regard either for the honourable or the
useful. Others, devoting themselves particularly to
the pursuit of gain, viz., the useful, pay less attention
to the honourable and the pleasurable. Others again
make honour their chief or only object of endeavour,
looking upon the useful and the delectable with com-
parative indifference. Now, we do nothing reprehen-

sible in desiring these things, provided we seek them there where alone they can be truly found. But where they are truly found, they are one. For the one Sovereign Good is at once supremely useful, supremely delectable, and supremely honourable. And this is our hope—so far as we can conceive it in the present life—and the promised vision, whereby we shall see in us the Divine Majesty : that God shall be all in all to us, all our pleasure, all our profit, all our honour. Amen.

SIXTH SERMON FOR CHRISTMAS EVE

On the Manner in which each of us should make himself a Bethlehem of Juda, so that Christ may be born in his Soul

" *Jesus Christ, the Son of God, is born in Bethlehem of Juda.*"—
From the *Martyrology*.

We have heard, my brethren, the announcement,
full of sweetness and "worthy of all acceptation,"
that, "Jesus Christ, the Son of God, is born in
Bethlehem of Juda." My very soul has melted at
the sound of these words, and my spirit is burning
in my bosom, eager with its usual ardour of desire
to communicate to you its own joy and exultation.
Jesus means Saviour. What is so necessary to the
lost as a saviour? What so welcome to the miserable?
To the despairing what so useful? For where could
we find salvation, where was there for us the faintest
hope of salvation under "the law of sin," in "the
malice of this day," in "the place of affliction," unless
it were born to us new and unexpected? Thou
perhaps, O my brother, desirest to be restored to
health, yet fearest the sharpness of the remedy, conscious of the desperate nature of thy disease and of
the tenderness of thy flesh. But take courage. Christ
is truly a Physician "sweet and mild, and plenteous
in mercy," because He it is Who has been "anointed
with the oil of gladness above His fellows," above
those, that is to say, who have received of the fulness
of His anointing, although not the fulness itself. But

lest thou shouldst imagine, from having heard Him
called sweet, that He will not be sufficiently powerful,
He is further declared to be the Son of God. For the
Son of God is equal to His Father and, like the Father,
can do whatsoever He wills.

Or perhaps, on being told about the utility of salvation and the sweetness of the saving unction, thou
mayest still feel unsatisfied, anxious, let me suppose,
concerning Christ's fittingness to be thy Saviour. As
the paralytic lying on his bed, or as the poor man
left half-dead on the way from Jerusalem to Jericho,
thou art glad to see the Saviour beside thee. Thy
gladness increases on discovering that He is not a
harsh Physician and uses no bitter remedies, for otherwise the short-lived pain of the cure might appear to
thee more intolerable than the continuance of the
malady. It is thus, my brethren, it is thus that many
even in our own time foolishly flee away from their
Physician and miserably perish, because although they
know Jesus, they know not Christ,* and so, after the
manner of men, estimate the sharpness of the remedies
prepared for them from the multitude and malignity
of their maladies. But now, if thou art certain as to
the presence of the Saviour, and knowest Him to be
Christ, Who makes use not of cauterants but of un-
guents, and heals by anointing rather than by burning,
—if thou art certain of this much, there remains still, as I
imagine, one more doubt which might possibly trouble
a creature of noble origin, lest perchance the Person

---

* That is to say, they know that the Incarnate Word has
the power to save them, since His name is Jesus, which means
Saviour ; but they fear He will be harsh with them, forgetting
that He is also called Christ, or the Anointed. Cf. Sermon
XXXVIII on the Canticle of Canticles.—(Translator.)

of the Saviour should seem not sufficiently worthy of thee. God forbid that any such thought should ever enter thy mind. But at all events, I do not suppose that thou hast so great an ambition and passion for glory, and art so desirous of honour, as that thou wouldst disdain to receive this grace of salvation, if it were offered thee by one of thy fellow-mortals. And were it offered thee by an angel, or an archangel, or by a saviour belonging to one of the higher angelic orders, thy fastidiousness would have still less reason to complain. As the case is, therefore, thou oughtest to receive the Saviour given thee with a devotion all the greater " as He hath inherited a more excellent name than they," and is called Jesus Christ, the Son of God. And see if the Angel who spoke to the shepherds and announced to them the " good tidings " of great joy, did not more clearly insinuate these three characteristics of our salvation, viz., its utility, its sweetness, and its dignity, when he said, " This day is born to you a Saviour, Who is Christ the Lord, in the city of David." Let us, therefore, my brethren, rejoice in this nativity, let us exult with gladness on this festival which the utility of salvation, the sweetness of the unction, and the Majesty of the Son of God so splendidly conspire to commend to us, that nothing is wanting to it of all that our hearts can desire. For it embraces in itself all manner of good, the useful, the delectable, and the honourable. Let us rejoice, I say, revolving in our minds and repeating to each other the sweet words, " Jesus Christ, the Son of God, is born in Bethlehem of Juda."

And let no undevout soul, no ungrateful and irreligious soul, make answer to this and say to me,

" This is nothing new. These tidings were announced long ages since. What thou hast been speaking of is an event of ancient date. Jesus Christ was born long ago." Yes, long ago and earlier still. This expression, " long ago and earlier still," will not surprise him who recalls the words of Moses, " The Lord shall reign for ever and beyond." Christ, therefore, was born not only before our time, but before all time. But this divine nativity " hath made darkness its covert," or perhaps I should rather say that it " dwelleth in light inaccessible." It lies concealed in the Bosom of the Father, as in a dark and mist-covered mountain. In order, therefore, that this, His eternal birth, might become known to us in some degree, He willed to have also a temporal generation. He was born in time of the flesh, and born in the flesh : for " the Word was made flesh." Yet it should be nothing surprising that even to this day the Church still announces, " Jesus Christ, the Son of God, is born in Bethlehem of Juda," since of the Same, long before His birth, it was said by the Prophet, " A Child is born to us." Long ago these tidings began to be heard and none of the saints has ever wearied of listening. For " Jesus Christ (is) yesterday, and to-day, and the same for ever." Hence the first man, Adam, the father of all the living, when proclaiming that great mystery, which the Apostle afterwards more clearly enunciated in reference to Christ and His Church, said, " Wherefore a man shall leave father and mother, and shall cleave to his wife, and they shall be two in one flesh." Hence Abraham also, the father of all the faithful, " rejoiced that he might see (this) day : he saw it and was glad." For why should

he have commanded his servant, when making him
" swear by the God of heaven and earth," to " put
his hand under his thigh," unless he foresaw that of
his seed the same God of heaven and earth was to
be born? *   God also revealed this secret counsel to
the " man according to His own Heart," who said,
" The Lord hath sworn truth to David and He will
not make it void : of the fruit of thy womb I will set
upon thy throne."   Therefore was Christ born in
Bethlehem of Juda, as the Angel testifies, in order
that the word of the Lord might be fulfilled and to
redeem the promises made to the fathers.   For Bethlehem of Juda is the city of David.   To the other
patriarchs and prophets likewise, " at sundry times
and in divers manners," the Lord made the same
announcement.   Heaven forbid the thought that it
was ever received with indifference by those true
lovers of God.   Do you think Moses was indifferent
when he said, " I beseech Thee, Lord, send Whom
Thou wilt send " ?   Or the Prophet Isaias, when he
exclaimed, " Oh, that Thou wouldst rend the heavens
and wouldst come down," and made use of many
other similar expressions ?   But " that which was
from the beginning " the holy apostles heard and saw
" and handled with their hands of the Word of life,"
for to them in particular it was said, " Blessed are the
eyes that see the things which you see."   Finally, for
us also, the faithful children of the Church, the same
blessedness has been preserved, sealed up, so to speak,
in the treasury of faith, according to the words of
Christ Himself, " Blessed are they that have not seen
and have believed."   This, my brethren, is our portion

* Cf. Genesis xxiv. 2-3.

in the Word of life. And assuredly it is nothing contemptible, since it communicates to us spiritual life and gives us the victory over the world. For it is written, "the just man liveth by faith," and "this is the victory which overcometh the world, our faith." Faith may be regarded as an image of eternity, comprehending, as it does, in its most ample bosom, all things past, present, and to come, so that nothing escapes it, nothing is lost to it, nothing lies beyond its range.

With good reason, therefore, did your hearts leap for joy, when the voice of this announcement sounded in your ears ; with good reason did you return thanks to God and prostrate yourselves on the floor in humble adoration,* lying together "under the shadow of His shoulders" and "hoping under His wings." Did not every one of you, on hearing the good tidings of the Saviour's nativity, repeat in his heart the words of the psalm, "It is good for me to adhere to my God, to put my hope in the Lord God"? Or rather these other words of the same Prophet, "Be thou, O my soul, subject to God"? But unhappy he,—if there be any such,—whose prostration has been an act of hypocrisy, whose heart was elated whilst his body was humbled. For as we read in Ecclesiastes, "There is one that humbleth himself wickedly, and his interior is full of deceit." Whosoever does not consider well his own necessities, whosoever does not feel his own defects, does not tremble at the dangers which surround him, does not devoutly run for help to the

---

* This custom still survives in the Cistercian Order. On Christmas Eve, when the religious who sings the martyrology in chapter announces the Feast of the Nativity, the whole community prostrate on the floor whilst they recite a Pater and Ave.—(Translator.)

new-born Saviour, does not lovingly subject himself to
God, nor gratefully sing with the Psalmist, " Lord,
Thou hast been our refuge " ; such a man's adoration
is not acceptable, his prostration is not sincere, his
humiliation has no value, his faith can give him neither
victory nor life.   Yet wherefore is it said, " Blessed
are they that have not seen and have believed " ?
For surely to believe in Christ is, at least in some sense,
to see Him ?   But consider carefully when and to whom
these words were spoken.   They were addressed to the
Apostle Thomas whom the Lord was reproving for that
he believed only because he had seen.   But it is not the
same thing to see and therefore to believe as to see by
believing.   For with respect to our father Abraham,
how can he be said to have seen the day of the Lord
except by believing ?   And how also are we to understand those other words which we sang in the office of
last night, " Sanctify yourselves to-day and be prepared,
for to-morrow you shall see in you the Majesty of
God "—how, I ask, is this to be understood, if it is
not true that we see with our souls whenever with
devout affection and " faith unfeigned " we represent
and recall to our minds that great " mystery of godliness which was manifested in the flesh, was justified
in the spirit, appeared unto angels, hath been preached
unto the gentiles, is believed in the world, is taken
up in glory " ?

   That, my brethren, is always new which always
renovates the mind.   That is never old which never
ceases to fructify, which no length of time can rob of
its freshness.   Such is this Holy One Whom God will
not "give to see corruption."   He is the new Man Who
is incapable of ever becoming old, and Who confers true

newness of life even upon those whose " bones have all grown old," as the Psalmist says.   Hence it is that in to-day's most sweet announcement, we are not told, as you may have noticed, that He *was* born, but that He *is* born, that " Jesus Christ, the Son of God, is born in Bethlehem of Juda."   For just as He is still daily immolated in a mystical manner whilst we " show forth His death " upon the altar, so also does He seem to be newly born whilst we annually commemorate His nativity.   To-morrow, therefore, we shall see the Majesty of God, not indeed in Himself but in us.   We shall see Majesty in humility, Power in weakness, God in man.   For He is Emmanuel, " which, being interpreted, is God with us."   But listen to a more evident testimony : " The Word was made flesh," writes St. John, " and dwelt among us."   Then and thereafter " we saw His glory, the glory, as it were, of the Only-Begotten of the Father, full of grace and truth." It was not the glory of divine power and Majesty that we saw, but the glory of the Father's love, the glory of His grace, whereof the Apostle says, " Unto the praise of the glory of His grace, in which He hath graced us in His beloved Son."

Thus, therefore, is He born.   But born where ? " In Bethlehem of Juda."   We must not, my brethren, pass over Bethlehem, for the shepherds did not say, " Let us *pass over* Bethlehem," but, " Let us pass over *to* Bethlehem."   What though it be but a poor insignificant village ?   What though it seems to be but " a little one among the thousands of Juda " ?   For such a birth-place is not unbefitting for Him Who, whereas He was rich, became poor for our sakes ; Who, although He was " the great Lord and greatly to be

praised," was born for us as a Little One ; Who said,
" Blessed are the poor in spirit, for theirs is the kingdom of heaven," and, " Unless you be converted and
become as little children, you shall not enter into the
kingdom of heaven." Therefore did He choose the
stable and the manger, a house of clay and the shelter
of beasts, in order to teach us that it is He Who
" lifteth up the poor out of the dunghill," and " pre-
serveth men and beasts."

Would to God that we also were each of us found
to be a Bethlehem of Juda, so that Christ might condescend to be born in us, and that we might deserve
to hear addressed to us the words, " Unto you that
fear My name the Sun of justice shall arise "! And
perhaps it is the same thing to say that a man must
make himself a Bethlehem of Juda if he would have
Jesus to be born in his heart, as what I remember to
have remarked awhile ago, namely, that there is need
of sanctification and preparation before we can see
in us the Majesty of God. For, according to the Royal
Prophet, " Judea is made His sanctification," because,
namely, all sins are washed away by confession ; * and
Bethlehem signifies the " house of bread," which seems
to be suggestive of preparation. How indeed is he
prepared to receive and entertain so noble a Guest,
who is obliged to say, " In my house there is no
bread " ? So we read of a certain man who, because
he was thus unprepared, had to go at midnight to a
neighbour's house and to knock at the closed door,
saying, " A friend of mine is come off his journey to me,
and I have not what to set before him." † " His heart

* The word Judea or Juda means confession, as has been
remarked in a preceding discourse.—(Translator.)
† Luke xi. 5-6.

is prepared to hope in the Lord," says the Psalmist, speaking no doubt of the just man, "his heart is strengthened, he shall not be moved." But the heart that is not strengthened cannot be prepared. Now we know on the testimony of the same Prophet, that it is bread which "strengtheneth man's heart." Not prepared, therefore, but "withered" and dry is my heart, if "I have forgotten to eat my bread." But "I am prepared and am not troubled, that I may keep the commandments" of life, if "forgetting the things that are behind, and stretching myself forth to those that are before, I press towards the mark." You observe, my brethren, that there is one kind of forgetfulness which is to be wished for, and another which we ought to avoid. For the whole tribe of Manasses * did not cross over the Jordan, nor did the whole tribe choose to remain on the hither side. There are some who forget the Lord their Creator, and there are some who "set Him always in their sight," forgetting their "people and their father's house." The former are oblivious of heavenly things, the latter of earthly ; the former of the future, the latter of the present ; the former of what is invisible, the latter of that which is seen ; the former of " the things of Jesus Christ," the latter of " the things that are their own." Both are Manasses, because both are forgetful : but the one is forgetful of Babylon, the other of Jerusalem. That is to say, the one is forgetful of what it is expedient to forget, and so is prepared ; the other, on the contrary, forgets what it is expedient to remember, inexpedient to forget, and he is altogether unprepared

* Cf. Josue xiii.-xvii. The word " Manasses " means oblivion. —(Translator.)

to see in himself the Majesty of God,—he is not a "house of bread" in which the Saviour will condescend to be born, nor is he the Manasses who has the vision of Him That ruleth over Israel and sitteth upon the cherubims, according to the Psalmist, "Thou That rulest Israel, Thou That sittest upon the cherubims, shine forth before Ephraim, Benjamin, and Manasses." In my opinion these three are the same who, according to the word of God, "shall deliver their souls by their justice," * and are called by the Prophet Ezechiel, Noe, Daniel, and Job. They are also represented, as I think, by the three † shepherds to whom, at the birth of the "Angel of the great counsel," the ministering angel announced great joy.

And consider further if you cannot recognise the same three, to wit, Ephraim, Benjamin, and Manasses, before whom God "shines forth," in the three Magi, who come now, not from the east alone, but "from the east and from the west" to "sit down with Abraham, Isaac, and Jacob, in the kingdom of heaven." And perhaps it will not seem unreasonable to suppose that to Ephraim (whose name signifies fructification) belongs the oblation of incense. For to "offer worthy incense for an odour of sweetness" is the office of those whom the Lord appointed that they "should go and bring forth fruit," that is, of the prelates of the Church. Benjamin, as being the "son of the right hand," has the duty of offering gold, that is, the substance of this world, in order that the faithful people, placed on the Judge's Right Hand, may deserve to hear, "I was hungry and you gave Me to eat, I was thirsty and you gave Me to drink." And Manasses,

* Cf. Ezechiel xiv. 13-14.　　† Cf. A Lapide in Luc. ii. 8.

if yet he desires that God should "shine forth" to him, must offer the myrrh of mortification, which, in my judgment, is particularly demanded from persons of our profession. I have said this in order to show that we do not belong to that part of the tribe of Manasses which remained on the hither side of the Jordan, but to the other which, "forgetting the things that are behind," stretches forward with eagerness to attain what lies before.

But now let us return to Bethlehem and let us see this Word Which is made, Which the Lord hath made and will show to us. It is good for us to be there, because Bethlehem, as I have already remarked, is the "house of bread." For where the Word of God is, there must also be the bread which "strengtheneth man's heart." Hence the Psalmist says, "Strengthen me in Thy Word." For man liveth "in the Word Which proceedeth from the Mouth of God," he liveth in Christ and Christ liveth in him. It is in the bread-strengthened heart that Christ is born and reveals Himself. He loves the heart which is strong and stable, not that which is weak and wavering. If any man hesitates, if any man falters, if any man murmurs, if any man purposes to wallow again in the mire, or to go back to the vomit, or to violate his vow, or to abandon his resolution, such a one cannot be called a Bethlehem, he is no "house of bread." It is only famine, and a very severe famine, that compels him to go down into Egypt, to feed the swine there, and to long for the husks which these poor animals eat : because he is far from the house of bread, far from the home of his Father, where, as he knows, even the "hired servants abound with bread." Christ, therefore, will not be born in such a heart as this, which is wanting in the strength of faith; for faith is the bread of life, as the Prophet Habacuc testifies where he says, " The just man liveth by faith." Hence the Apostle also assures us that so long as we live here below, Christ, Who is the true Life of our souls, " dwelleth by faith in our hearts." How indeed could Jesus be born there, how could salvation be found in the inconstant heart, since the word of the Lord stands firm and fixed, that only " he that shall persevere unto the end, he shall be saved "? And that the man of wavering will has not Christ within him and is not of the number of those to whom it is said, " You have the unction from the Holy One," is manifest from this especially, that his " heart is withered " because (he) forgot to eat (his) bread." Much less can such a one belong to the Son of God, Whose Spirit, as the Prophet Isaias bears witness, will only rest upon " him that is poor and little, and of a contrite heart, and that trembleth at (His) words." Besides, there can be no fellowship between eternal fixedness and such muta-bility, between Him Who is, and him " who never continueth in the same state." Nevertheless, however constant we may be, however strong in faith, however well prepared, however abounding with bread through the mercy of Him to Whom we daily cry, " Give us this day our daily bread " : in spite of all this, we still have need to add the petition which follows in the Lord's Prayer, " And forgive us our trespasses." For " if we say that we have no sin, we deceive ourselves and the truth is not in us." He is this Truth, Who is born not simply in Bethlehem, but in Bethlehem of Juda, Jesus Christ, the Son of God.

Therefore, my brethren, " let us come before (the Lord's) presence with confession," so that being both sanctified and prepared, we also may be found to be, each one of us, a Bethlehem of Juda, and thus may deserve to see the Saviour born in us. But—and this is a matter of much importance for ourselves—if any soul should have made such progress that she is now a fruitful virgin, that she is now a star of the sea, that she is now full of grace and has the Holy Spirit coming down upon her, I believe that He will condescend to be born not only *in* but even *of* such a soul. Yet no one should presume to claim for himself so great a privilege save those whom He has Himself particularly designated and pointed out, as it were, with His finger, where He says, " Behold My mother and My brethren." * And listen to one of these mystical mothers : " My little children," exclaims St. Paul, " of whom I am in labour again, until Christ be formed in you." For if Christ seemed to be born in the disciples whilst He was being formed in them, why may I not also presume to say that Christ was born of the Apostle, by whom He was in a manner brought forth in them ? It is thou, O impious Synagogue, it is thou that hast brought forth to us this Child, discharging the office of a mother, yet without a mother's affection. Thou didst put Him out of thy womb, didst drive Him

* Compare the following from Faber : " Oh, think of those mighty words in the Gospel : The same is My brother, My sister, and My mother ! Only let us do God's will and we are all Maries, and angels will hail us, and Christ will be born of us, and though His cross may cause us seven and seven times seven sorrows, yet at the last He will assume us into heaven and crown us there, doing to us in our measure what He has done to Mary in her measure " (*Life and Letters*, p. 273).—(Translator.)

forth from thy city, and, lifting Him above the earth, didst seem to say to the Church of the gentiles and to the primeval Church, which is in heaven, " Let Him belong neither to you nor to me, but let Him be divided. Let Him be divided not *between* both, but *from* both." For after expelling Him from the city, and raising Him up (so that He might remain neither within thy walls nor upon the earth) thou didst compass Him about with a palisade of iron to prevent His escape on this side or on that. O most cruel mother, how couldst thou have the heart thus to cast forth the Child of thy womb with none to receive or to care Him ? Look now and see how much thou hast gained by thy cruelty, or rather how thou hast gained nothing at all. For everywhere the daughters of Sion are going forth to see King Solomon in the diadem wherewith thou, His mother, hast crowned Him. But He, leaving His mother, hath cleaved to His Bride, and they are two in one flesh. Banished from Jerusalem and lifted up from the earth, He is drawing all things to Himself because He is the Same Who is over all things, God blessed for ever. Amen.

SERMONS FOR CHRISTMAS DAY

FIRST SERMON FOR CHRISTMAS DAY

On the Fountains of the Saviour

" You shall draw waters with joy out of the Saviour's fountains, and you shall say in that day : Praise ye the Lord and call upon His name."—Isaias xii. 2-3.

Truly great, my dearest brethren, is the festival we keep to-day in honour of the Lord's nativity. But the shortness of the time at our disposal admits of only a short sermon. Nor ought you to be surprised that I shorten my words, seeing that God the Father has to-day shortened * His own Word. Shall I tell you how extended was that Divine Word, and how much He has been contracted ? " Do not I fill heaven and earth ? saith the Lord," by His Prophet Jeremias. But now, made flesh, He lies in a narrow manger. Again, the Psalmist says to Him, " From eternity and to eternity Thou art God." And see ! He has become as an Infant of a day. Wherefore, brethren, or by what necessity has the Lord of Majesty so humbled Himself, so emptied Himself, so " shortened " Himself, unless it be in order to induce us to do likewise ? And thus He now already preaches by His example what He shall later on proclaim with His lips : " Learn of Me because I am meek and humble of heart." Hence we find it written in the Acts of the Apostles that " Jesus began to do and to teach." I beg of

* Allusion to Romans ix. 28.

125

you, then, dearest brethren, and most earnestly beseech you not to allow so noble an example to be
presented to you without profiting by it, but rather
to make it your model and to " be renewed in
the spirit of your minds." Be diligent in acquiring
humility, which is the foundation and the guardian of
the virtues. Cultivate humility, because by it alone
can you save your souls. What indeed could be more
unworthy, what more detestable, what deserving of
severer chastisement than that man should still " presume to magnify himself upon the earth " after seeing
the God of heaven making Himself so little ? It is
intolerable impudence on the part of a wretched little
worm to inflate and enlarge itself, when the Lord of
glory has voluntarily laid aside His greatness.

This, then, is the reason why He Who " in the form
of God " was equal to the Father, yet " emptied
Himself, taking the form of a servant." But He only
emptied Himself of His Majesty and His power, not
also of His goodness and mercy. For what says the
Apostle ? " The goodness and kindness of God our
Saviour appeared." Already He had exhibited His
power in the creation of the world ; His wisdom was
constantly revealed in the government of the universe ;
but His goodness and kindness became especially
manifest in His incarnation. His power was made
known to the Jews in signs and wonders. Hence in
their law we frequently find the words, " I, the Lord,"
" I, the Lord." The philosophers likewise, " abounding
in their own sense," had knowledge of His Majesty,
because, as the Apostle bears witness, " That which
is known of God is manifest in them." Nevertheless,
the Jews were oppressed by the power which they

knew, and the philosophers, becoming " searchers of Majesty," were " overwhelmed by glory." For power demands subjection, Majesty calls for admiration, whilst imitation belongs to neither. Therefore, let Thy good- ness, O Lord, appear, to which man, who is made to Thy image, may be conformed. Thy Majesty, Thy power, and Thy wisdom it is not possible for us to imitate, nor is it expedient to emulate. But how long shall Thy mercy confine itself to a part of Thy angelic creation, leaving the rest, along with the whole human race, to be occupied by Thy justice? " O Lord, Thy mercy is in heaven, and Thy truth, viz., Thy justice, reacheth even unto the clouds," condemning all the earth, together with the powers of the air. But let Thy mercy widen its boundaries; let it extend its do- main; let it expand its bosom ; let it " reach from end to end mightily and dispose all things sweetly." Thou art straitened, O Lord, within the compass of Thy justice ; put off Thy girdle and come down to us flowing with mercies, overflowing with charity.

And thou, O man, why art thou fearful ? Wherefore dost thou tremble " before the Face of the Lord because He cometh " ? For He is coming to save the world, not to judge it. Long ago thou wert induced by a faithless fellow-servant to steal the royal diadem and to place it upon thy head. But thou wert dis- covered in the act. Good reason hadst thou then to be afraid. Good reason hadst thou then to flee from the Face of the Lord. For perhaps He was already brandishing the flaming sword. Now, however, in a land of exile, thou eatest thy bread in the sweat of thy brow, and behold, a voice is heard on the earth proclaiming the coming of the Lord. Whither shalt thou go from His Spirit? Or whither shalt thou flee from His Face? But do not fear, do not fly. He comes not now in anger. He seeks thee not for punishment but in order to save thee. And lest on this occasion also thou shouldst say, " I heard Thy voice and I hid myself," behold He has become an Infant, a little speechless Babe. For His wailing cries should rather move thee to compassion than inspire thee with terror: and even if perchance there be some others to whom they are a cause of alarm, surely they are not so to thee. He has made Himself a Little One; His Virgin Mother wraps Him in His poor swaddling clothes: and art thou still fearful and trembling? This alone should convince thee that He comes not to destroy but to save thee, to deliver and not to bind thee, the fact, namely, that He is already fighting against thy foes, that He, as the Power and the Wisdom of God, is already trampling on the necks of the proud and haughty demons.

Thou, O man, hast two enemies, sin and death, that is to say, the death of the soul and the death of the body. Christ is come to conquer both, and from both will He save thee. Only be not afraid. Even already He has vanquished sin in His own Person by taking upon Himself our human nature, free from all defilement. For great violence was done to sin, and it manifestly sustained a heavy defeat, when that very nature which it boasted of having entirely corrupted and completely subdued, was found in Christ wholly reclaimed from it. After this first victory, He " will pursue after (thy) enemies and overtake them, and (He) will not turn back again till they are consumed." Fighting against sin during His mortal existence, He will oppose it with His words and example ; in His passion He will bind it, He will bind " the strong man and plunder his house." Then, as regards death, He will in the same manner and order vanquish it first in Himself, when He rises from the tomb, " the first-fruits of them that sleep," " the First-Begotten of the dead." Afterwards He will overcome it in us also, when He will raise up again our mortal bodies : so shall our enemy, death, be at last destroyed. Therefore will He be " clothed with beauty " at His resurrection, not, as now in His nativity, wrapped in swaddling clothes. Therefore He whose Heart is now brimming over with mercy, Who now judgeth no man, will then, at His rising, gird Himself, and with the cincture of justice will seem to restrain, so to speak, the flowing robes of His mercy. For from that time He shall be prepared for the judgment, which is reserved for our resurrection. And therefore He comes now as a Little One, in order to give mercy the precedence, and that mercy, going before, may temper the severity of the final judgment which must follow.

Yet, although He has come to us now as a Little One, not little but great are the blessings He has brought and bestowed upon us. Would you like to know what these are ? Well, in the first place He has brought us mercy, the mercy according to which " He has saved us," as the Apostle testifies. For Christ is for us as a fountain, in which we may wash ourselves clean, as it is written, " Who hath loved us and washed us from our sins." But this is not the only use of water : it can serve us in more ways than by washing out our stains. Thus it can also quench our thirst. " Blessed is the man," says Holy Scripture,

" that shall continue in wisdom, and that shall meditate in his justice," and a little further on, " With the
bread of life and understanding she (justice) shall feed
him and give him the water of wholesome wisdom to
drink." Well does the Holy Spirit describe this wisdom
as wholesome, since " the wisdom of the flesh is death,"
and the wisdom of the world also is " an enemy to
God." The only wholesome wisdom is that which
comes from God, and which, according to St. James,
is " first indeed chaste, then peaceable." But the
wisdom of the flesh is impure instead of chaste, and
the wisdom of the world is rather contentious than
peaceable. The wisdom which is from God is chaste,
in that it seeks not the things that are its own but
" the things that are Jesus Christ's," so that, instead
of letting us follow each his own will, it makes us
consider what is the will of God. And, it is peaceable
inasmuch as it does not "abound in its own sense," but
rather acquiesces in the judgment and counsel of others.

A third use of water is for irrigation, of which young
plants especially have the greatest need. Without it
they will either perish entirely or their growth will be
greatly retarded for want of moisture. Whoever,
therefore, has sown the seeds of good works should
seek for the water of devotion, so that, irrigated from
the fountain of grace, the garden of his virtuous life may
not wither but may flourish in a never-fading bloom.
It is for such a soul the Psalmist is praying when he
says, " And may thy whole burnt-offering be made
fat." Thus also is it written in praise of Aaron that
a heavenly fire daily consumed his sacrifice. From
this, so it seems, we are to understand that our
good works ought to be seasoned with the fervour of

devotion and with the sweetness of spiritual grace. Do
you think it possible to find a fourth use of water,
or let me say, a fourth fountain, so that we may be
able to recover that paradise which was watered and
beautified by a four-branched stream ? * For if we
despair of having the earthly paradise restored to us,
how can we hope for the kingdom of heaven ? " If
I have spoken to you earthly things," said the Saviour,
" and you believe not ; how will you believe if I shall
speak to you heavenly things ? " As it is, however, in
order that the bestowal of present favours may confirm
our hope of the future kingdom, we already actually
possess a much better and more delightful Paradise
than the one which our first parents lost ; and this
Paradise of ours is none other than Christ the Lord.
In this living Paradise we have now discovered three
of the fountains, and the fourth is yet to seek. We
have the waters of pardon from the fountain of mercy
to wash away our sins ; we have the waters of prudence from the fountain of wisdom to slake our thirst ;
and we have the waters of devotion from the fountain
of grace to irrigate the plants of our good works. Let
us now seek for the heated waters of ardent zeal with
which to cook our food. For these waters serve both to
spiritualise and to warm our affections, and they flow
from the fountain of charity. Hence the Psalmist says,
" My heart grew hot within me, and in my meditation
a fire shall flame out " ; and in another place, " The
zeal of Thy house hath eaten me up." For the sweetness of devotion engenders the love of justice, and the
fervour of zeal a hatred of iniquity. And see if the
Prophet Isaias is not alluding to these fountains where
he says, " You shall draw waters with joy out of the

* Cf. Genesis ii. 10.

Saviour's fountains." But in order to understand that this promise is to be fulfilled, not in the future life, but in the present, consider the words which follow, " And you shall say in that day : Praise ye the Lord and call upon His name." Now it is only in this life that we are to invoke the name of God, because He has said through the Psalmist, " Call upon Me in the day of trouble."

Furthermore, of these four fountains, the second, third, and fourth appear to belong to the three orders in the Church, one to each. The first is common to all, " for in many things we all offend," and consequently have need of the fountain of mercy to wash away the defilement of our transgressions. " All have sinned," says the Apostle, " and do need the glory, that is, the mercy, of God " ; and to whichever order we may belong, whether we are prelates, virgins, or married men, " if we say that we have no sin, we deceive ourselves and the truth is not in us." Therefore, since " no one is free from stain," the fountain of mercy is necessary for all, and all alike, Noe, Daniel, and Job,* ought to run to its waters with the same eagerness. With regard to the other three fountains, let Job seek especially that of wisdom, because he, more than others, walks in the midst of snares, so that it will be a wonderful thing if he avoids all evil. Daniel must have recourse to the fountain of grace, for he has need to irrigate his penitential labours and the austerity of his abstinence with the grace of devotion. It is necessary that we in particular should do everything with cheerfulness, since

* These three holy men are taken as types of the three orders referred to, Noe representing the prelates (Gen. viii. 20), Daniel the virgins, and Job those engaged in the married state.— (Translator.)

" God loveth a cheerful giver." For this earth of ours produces now but very little of the seed of good works, and that little easily perishes unless it be watered with repeated irrigations. Hence in the Lord's Prayer, we daily solicit this grace of devotion when we ask for our daily bread. And not without reason, since otherwise we might fall under that terrible malediction pronounced by the Prophet, " Let them be as grass upon the tops of houses, which withereth before it be plucked up." But to Noe belongs in a special manner the fountain of zeal, because the zeal of charity is looked for particularly in prelates.

Therefore, my brethren, to us who are still living in the flesh, Christ exhibits in Himself four fountains. And He promises after this our exile, to give us a fifth, namely, the fountain of life, for which the Psalmist thirsted when he sang, " My soul hath thirsted after the strong living God." Perhaps it was to designate the first four fountains that Christ was wounded in four places whilst He hung yet living on the cross ; and the opening of His Side after He had yielded up His Spirit, may have been intended to signify the fifth. He was still alive when they pierced His Hands and His Feet, so that He might allow four fountains to flow forth from Himself unto us, who are also still living. The fifth wound was inflicted after He had expired, in order that for us, after our death, the fifth fountain might be opened. But behold ! Whilst discoursing on the mysteries of the Lord's nativity, I have suddenly digressed to contemplate those of His passion. However, you must not be surprised that I seek in His passion for what He brought us at His birth. For it was in His passion that the coffer was broken and the treasure it contained poured out as the price of our redemption.

SECOND SERMON FOR CHRISTMAS DAY

On the Three Principal Works of God, and the Special Virtue conspicuous in each

" The Lord hath done great things for us."—Ps. cxxv. 3.

" Great are the works of the Lord," cries out the Prophet David. All God's works are great indeed, my brethren, because He is Himself so great. But those which appear to be the greatest amongst them have a special relation to ourselves. Hence it is that the same Prophet declares in one of the psalms, " The Lord hath done great things for us." And there are three of His works particularly which proclaim aloud how magnificently He has dealt with us. These are, the work of our first creation, the work of our present redemption, and the work of our future glorification. But how many great operations, O Lord, does not each of the three comprise! To Thee it belongs to " shew forth to Thy people the power of Thy works," but concerning the works themselves we must not be silent. In each of the three works of creation, redemption, and glorification, we have to consider a special union or blending of opposite elements, truly worthy of the divine power and efficacy. In the first work of our creation, " God formed man of the slime of the earth, and breathed into his face the breath of life." Oh, what an Artist, what a Compounder of things diverse, at Whose command the slime of the earth and the spirit of life are thus intimately wedded together! The slime indeed had already received existence, when " in the beginning

God created heaven and earth." But the spirit had a creation proper to itself. It was not produced in common with other things. Neither was it created in the bodily mass, but was infused into it in a singular and excellent manner. Acknowledge, O man, thy dignity. Acknowledge the glory of thy human nature. Thou hast a body like other earthly creatures, since it is only fitting that, as thou art set over all the material world, thou shouldst resemble it at least in part. But thou art also possessed of something more sublime, something which lifts thee entirely above the level of other visible beings. For in thee are united and compacted together spirit and flesh, the former infused, the latter fashioned from the slime.

But for the sake of which element are they thus combined? Which of the two gains by their partnership? According to the wisdom of the children of this world, whenever there is an alliance between high and low, he that is stronger obtains the dominion and uses for his pleasure his weaker associate. The more powerful trample upon the less powerful, the learned laugh at the ignorant, the crafty deceive the simple, the mighty contemn the feeble. But it is not so in Thy works, O Lord; it is not so in this union which Thou hast made. It is not for the sole advantage of the superior partner Thou hast associated the slime of the earth with the spirit of life, the lofty with the lowly, a noble and excellent creature with a mass of vile and worthless clay. For who does not know how much the soul benefits the body? What would the body be without the soul but a lifeless trunk? To the soul it owes its beauty, to the soul it owes its increase and development, to the soul it owes its clearness of vision and the sound of its voice : in fine, it owes to the soul all its various powers of sensation. This union speaks to me of charity. I thus find the record of charity in the very page which tells me of my own creation. For the Creator has not only announced to me the law of charity at the very commencement of my career, but with His own Hand He has lovingly inscribed it on my being and substance.

Truly great, my dearest brethren, was this alliance of spirit and flesh, if only it had continued firm. As a matter of fact, however, notwithstanding that it had been strengthened with the divine seal (for God made man to His own image and likeness) the seal was broken and the union, alas ! destroyed. When as yet that seal was fresh and new, the infernal robber came and broke it. The divine image having been thus lost, miserable man is now " compared to senseless beasts and is become like to them." God made man righteous, and so stamped upon him His own likeness, the likeness of Him of whom the Psalmist sings, " The Lord our God is righteous and there is no iniquity in Him." He also made him truthful and just, as He Himself is Truth and Justice. Nor could the union between flesh and spirit be dissolved whilst this seal of likeness remained unbroken. But there appeared an impostor, who, promising our unsuspecting first parents a better seal, alas! alas! destroyed that which had been impressed by the Hand of God. " You shall be as gods," whispered the serpent, "knowing good and evil." O malevolent one ! O most wicked one ! What advantage can it be to them to resemble their Creator by such knowledge ? Let them by all means be as gods : let them be truthful as God is truthful, to Whom

sin can never approach. For so long as the seal of
such likeness endures, the original union of soul and
body is safe. But we know now from experience to
what we have been persuaded by the deceit of the
devil's craft. For when the seal had been violated,
there followed bitter dissension between the partners
and lamentable divorce. Where now, O impious one,
where now is thy promise, " You shall not die the
death"? For behold we all die, so that the Psalmist
says, " Who is the man that shall live and not see
death ? "

But what wilt Thou do, O Lord our God? Is this
work of Thine never to be repaired ? Shall not he
who has fallen be assisted to rise ? But there is none
that can help him except the Lord Who created him.
Therefore, "By reason of the misery of the needy and
the groans of the poor, now will I arise, saith the
Lord "; and " The enemy shall have no advantage
over him, nor the son of iniquity have power to hurt
him." " I will form another union," He seems to
say, " which I will secure with a stronger and deeper
Seal, with that, namely, Which is not something made
to My Image, but is Itself My Image, the Figure of
My Substance and the Splendour of My Glory, a Seal
not made but begotten before the day-star." And
lest you should have any fears that this new Seal may
be broken like the other, listen to the Prophet speaking
thereof, " My strength," he says in one of the psalms,
" is dried up, viz., hardened, like a potshred." Yes,
" like a potshred," but such a potshred as Satan, the
mighty hammer of the whole earth, has no power to
break. The first union was an alliance of two, the
second is a conjunction of three, suggesting to us a

resemblance to the mystery of the Most Holy Trinity. The Word Who "was in the beginning with God" and " was God "; the Soul Which had been created out of nothing and before was not ; and the Flesh Which divine wisdom separated from the mass of corruption and preserved undefiled : these three elements have coalesced in the unity of a single Person, and are bound together with an indissoluble bond. In this union we find a threefold manifestation of power : that which was not has been created; that which had perished has been restored ; that which was over all things has been " made a little less than the angels." These three ingredients, my brethren, are symbolised by the " three measures of meal," which, as the Gospel tells us, were leavened together, and made into the " Bread of angels " whereof man eateth, the Bread Which " strengtheneth man's heart." Happy that woman, and blessed amongst all women, in whose chaste bosom this heavenly Bread was baked, baked over the fire of the Holy Spirit. Blessed, I say, is that woman who hid the leaven of her faith in these three measures. For it was by faith she conceived and by faith she brought forth. To this St. Elizabeth bears witness when she says, " Blessed art thou that hast believed, because those things shall be accomplished that were spoken to thee by the Lord." And be not surprised to hear that it was by means of Mary's faith that the Word was united to flesh, because it was from Mary's flesh Christ's Flesh was taken. Nor is it any objection to this interpretation that, according to the Gospel, "the kingdom of heaven is like to leaven." For, as it seems to me, the faith of Mary may also be likened to the kingdom of heaven, since it was by her faith the kingdom of heaven has been restored.

Therefore no creature has power to break the bond of this second union, since even " the prince of this world hath not anything " he can claim in Christ, and the Baptist is not worthy to loose the latchet of His shoe. What then ? It is plainly needful that it be dissolved to some extent. Otherwise the first union, which has been destroyed, can never be restored. Bread that is unbroken, a treasure that is concealed, wisdom that is not manifest—what is the use of such things ? With good reason did St. John weep, as he tells us in the Apocalypse, " because no man was found worthy to open the book and to loose the seals thereof." For whilst it remained closed none of us could gain access to the divine wisdom it contained. Open Thou the book, O Lamb of God, O Thou Who art meekness itself. Present Thy Hands and Thy Feet to the Jew, to be pierced with nails, so that the treasure of salvation, the " plentiful redemption " concealed within, may at last pour itself out. " Break Thy bread to the hungry," because Thou alone canst break it Who alone art able to stand in order to repair Thy broken creatures. For in the general breaking * Thou alone dost possess the power to lay down Thy life and to take it up again when Thou pleasest. Therefore, in Thy compassion for our need, let this Temple be dissolved in part, but not utterly destroyed. Let the Soul be separated from the Body, but let the Divinity guard the incorruption of the Flesh, and confer upon the Spirit full liberty, so that It alone may be " free among the dead " to lead forth from

* Allusion to Psalm cv. 23.

their prison-house them that are shut up and sitting in darkness and in the shadow of death. Let Thy holy Soul lay aside Its immaculate Flesh, but only to take It up again on the third day, so that by dying Thou mayest destroy death, and by rising from the dead mayest restore life to man. So it has been, dearest brethren, and it is a cause of joy to us that it has so been. Death has been slain by His death, and we have been " regenerated unto the hope of life by the resurrection of Jesus Christ from the dead."

But as for the third union, who shall describe it ? " Eye hath not seen, nor ear heard, neither hath it entered into the heart of man what things God hath prepared for them that love Him." That will be the consummation, when Christ shall " deliver up the kingdom to God and the Father," and they, viz., Christ and His Bride, the Church, shall be two, not now in one flesh, but in one spirit. For if the Word by cleaving to the flesh was made flesh, much more shall she that cleaves to God become one spirit with Him. In the second union of the Word with flesh, humility is manifested, a humility exceedingly great. But in that for which we look, for which we sigh, there is laid up for us—if indeed for us—the perfection of heavenly glory. If you recall now what I said about the first of these unions, in which man is compacted of spirit and flesh, namely, that therein charity is commended to us, you will see with what reason humility is so conspicuous in the second, because it is only the virtue of humility that can repair the injury done to charity. The union of such a noble creature as the rational soul with a body fashioned from the slime of the earth, must not be ascribed to humility. For it is not by its own deliberate choice that the spirit is mixed with matter, since it is infused by the very act which creates it and created by the very act which infuses it.* But the same is not true of the Sovereign and Divine Spirit, Who being infinitely good, has united Himself by His own free will and pleasure to a Body pure and undefiled. Then the union of glory follows upon that of charity and humility ; because without charity nothing is of any avail, and, according to the words of Christ, no one shall be exalted but he that humbleth himself.

---

* " Creando immittur, immitendo creatur." By these few words the Saint excludes all the various false theories touching the origin of the human soul : the traducianism of Tertullian, according to which the infant's soul is derived by material generation from the bodies of the parents ; the more spiritual but equally unintelligible traducianism to which St. Augustine inclined, and which Frohshammer and Klee resuscitated in Germany at the beginning of the last century, viz., that the soul of the offspring proceeds somehow from the souls of the parents ; the theory of Origen who, influenced by Plato's philosophy, and misinterpreting Ps. xxxii. 15, taught that all souls were created together at the beginning of time ; and finally the strange doctrine of Rosmini, that the sentient soul, produced by generation, is in man transformed into a rational, spiritual soul " by the manifestation to it of the idea of being." The teaching of St. Bernard is the teaching of the Catholic Church : that the human soul does not exist before its union with the body, and that it is produced by creation out of nothing. Cf. Maher, *Psychology*, 572-4 ; Hickey, *Summula*, vol. ii. 456-9 ; also Bellarmin, *Comment. in Ps.* xxxii. 15.—(Translator.)

THIRD SERMON FOR CHRISTMAS DAY

On the Place, Time, and other circumstances of the Nativity

" The Word was made flesh and dwelt among us."—John i. 14.

In the nativity of Christ, my brethren, we have to consider two orders of things, two orders which are not only distinct from each other, but very much unlike. To the first belong the birth of a Child Who is very God; the preservation of His Mother's virginity; and the painlessness of her bringing forth. To the same: the new light from heaven shining amid the darkness; the Angel's announcement of tidings of great joy; the multitude of the heavenly host singing praises to their King; glory given to God in the highest and on earth peace to men of good will; the shepherds hastening to Bethlehem, and finding there the Word announced to them, and telling the news to others; the awe and admiration of everyone that hears. These and all such-like happenings, my dearest brethren, are the work of divine power, not of human weakness. They are, as it were, plates and vessels of silver and gold, from which even the poor are allowed to eat and drink to-day at the table of the Lord, on account of the greatness of the solemnity. But we have no permission to take them away: it is not the golden dish and goblet that are given us, but the food and drink they contain. "When thou shalt sit to eat with a prince," says the Wise Man, "consider diligently what is set before thy face." But—to come to the things of

the second order—I recognise as truly my own the time
and place of this nativity, the tenderness of the Infant's
Body, the cries and tears of the Little One ; also the
poverty and the night-watches of the shepherds to whom
the Saviour's birth is first announced. These things, I
say, are mine ; they serve my interests ; they are the
food set before me ; they are given me for my instruc-
tion and consolation. Christ was born in winter, and
He was born at night. Are we to suppose, my brethren,
that it was by mere chance and without any special design, that He to Whom belong day and night, summer
and winter, came into this world in the most inclement
of seasons and in the time of darkness? Other infants
do not choose the time of their birth, because, hardly
yet beginning to live, they have not the use of reason
or the faculty of free choice, or the power of delibera-
tion. But Christ, although He was not man before
His incarnation, nevertheless " was in the beginning
with God " and " was God," possessing the same wisdom
and power as now, as being always the Wisdom and
the Power of God. Consequently, when the Son of
God was about to be born into this world, it was
His privilege to choose whatever season He pleased.
And the choice He made was of the most disagreeable,
especially for a little Child, the Son of a poor Mother,
who had scarcely the swaddling clothes in which to
wrap Him, and no cradle wherein to lay Him but the
manger. Nowhere can I find any mention of furs for
His use, although the necessity was undoubtedly great.
The first Adam covered himself with garments of skins ;
the second Adam is wrapped in poor swaddling clothes.
Such things, my brethren, are not in accordance with
he wisdom of the world. Therefore either Jesus Christ

is deceived or the world is in error.   But it is impossible that He Who is the Wisdom of God should be
liable to deception.   Justly then is the prudence of
the flesh—which is death—called " an enemy to God,"
and the wisdom of the world " foolishness."   For consider.   Christ, Whose judgment is infallible, has chosen
for Himself what is most disagreeable to nature.   This
must, consequently, be better, more expedient, more
desirable than what pleases the flesh.   And should any
one teach or recommend to you a different doctrine,
avoid him as a seducer.

The Saviour also selected the night as the time of
His birth.   Where now are those who so shamelessly
desire to make a parade of themselves ?   Christ chooses
what He judges to be most salutary : you select what
He repudiates.   Is your wisdom superior to his ?   Is your
judgment more true than His ?   Is your decision safer
than His ?   Christ holds His peace, He does not extol
Himself.   He does not magnify or preach Himself ; and
behold an angel announces Him, whilst a multitude of
the heavenly host celebrates His advent.   Do thou, therefore, my brother, if thou wouldst follow Christ, conceal the
treasure which thou hast found.   Love to be unknown.*
Let another's mouth praise thee, but thine own never.
Furthermore, Christ was born in a stable and laid in
a manger.   But is it not He Who says, " Mine is the
earth and the fulness thereof " ?   Wherefore, then,
does He choose a stable ?   Evidently in order to condemn the glory of this world, to reprobate the vanity
of men.   As yet His tongue is silent, but all else that
belongs to Him cries aloud, preaches, evangelises.   Even

* " If thou wouldst know and learn anything to the purpose,
love to be unknown " (*Imitation of Christ*, Bk. I. ch. ii.).

the limbs of His infant Body have the power of utter-
ance. In everything does He censure, oppose, and
refute the judgment of the world. For who amongst
men, if given the choice, would not rather select a strong
body and fully developed faculties than the tenderness
and helplessness of childhood ? O Wisdom, " drawn out
of secret places," as holy Job says ! O Wisdom of God
truly incarnated and veiled under the flesh ! For in truth,
my brethren, this Child is the Little One promised of
old through Isaias, Who should " know to refuse the
evil and to choose the good." Bodily comfort must
therefore be evil, and affliction of the flesh must be good,
since this wise Little One, this infant Word chooses the
latter and rejects the former. For " the Word was
made flesh," weak flesh, infant flesh, tender flesh, feeble
flesh, flesh incapable of any work, of any labour.

And truly, my brethren, " the Word was made
flesh and dwelt (in the flesh) among us." Whilst He
" was in the beginning with God " He dwelt in " light
inaccessible," and there was none able to endure His
brightness, " for who hath known the mind of the
Lord ? Or who hath been His counsellor ? " " The
sensual man perceived not these things that are of the
Spirit of God." But now even " the sensual man "
may perceive, because the Word is made flesh. If he
can comprehend nothing but what concerns the flesh,
behold the Word is now flesh : let him hear that Word
even in the flesh. O man, the Wisdom of God is presented to thee in the flesh. That Wisdom which was
formerly concealed, behold It is now " drawn out of
(Its) secret places," and manifests Itself even to thy
bodily senses. It calls out to thee, as I may say, in a
manner intelligible even to the carnal-minded, " Shun

pleasure, because death sits close to the entrance of
delight.   Do penance, because by penance the kingdom
of heaven is brought near."   This, my brethren, this is
what the stable preaches to us, this is what the manger
clearly expresses, what those infantine members unmis-
takably announce, what those tears and cries proclaim
aloud.   Christ weeps, but not as other children are wont
to weep, I mean not for the same reason.   For it is sensible suffering that causes the tears in others, whereas
the tears of Christ flow from an affection of compassion.
Other infants weep because of their own misery, Christ
weeps over ours.   They lament the heavy burden which
weighs upon all the children of Adam, He bewails the
sins which defile the children of Adam.   And for those
for whom He now pours out His tears, He will hereafter shed His Blood.   Oh, the flinty hardness of this
heart of mine !   Would to God that it also, like the
Word, was made flesh !   Thou, O Lord, hast even promised this by Thy Prophet Ezechiel, saying, " I will
take away the stony heart out of their flesh, and will
give them a heart of flesh."

Brethren, the tears of Christ overwhelm me with shame
and fear and sorrow.   I was playing out of doors in the
street, whilst sentence of death was being passed upon
me in the privacy of the royal council-chamber.   But
the King's only-begotten Son heard of it.   And what
did He do ?   He went forth from the palace, put off
His diadem, covered Himself with sackcloth, strewed
ashes on His head, bared His feet, and wept and lamented
because His poor slave was condemned to death.   I
meet Him unexpectedly in this sad condition.   I am
astonished at the woeful change in Him and inquire the
cause.   He tells me the whole story.   What am I to do

now? Shall I continue to play and make a mockery of
His tears? Surely I have neither sense nor reason if I
do not rather follow Him and unite my tears with His.
This is the cause of my shame. Shall I tell you also
the source of my sorrow and my fear? It is the fact
that I estimate the magnitude of my danger from a
consideration of the remedy. I had no idea how desperate was my condition. I believed myself to be in
good health. And behold, the Son of the Virgin, the
Son of the Most High, is sent for, and ordered to be
slain, so that my wounds may be healed by the balsam
of His most precious Blood! Acknowledge, O man,
how serious were thy wounds, since to heal them it
was necessary that Christ should be wounded. Had
thy wounds not been unto death, yea, unto everlasting
death, the Son of God would never have died for their
remedy. It were shame for us, then, dearest brethren,
to neglect or dissemble those wounds of ours for which
we behold so august a Majesty manifesting so much
compassion. The Son of God compassionates our
misery and weeps over us, and shall we who suffer
the misery, only laugh at it? Thus the consideration
of the preciousness of the remedy fills my soul with
fear and sorrow.

Nevertheless, this very fact of the remedy being so
precious shall also become to me a source of consolation, if I am faithful in carrying out the Doctor's pre-
scriptions. For if, on the one hand, the use of such
costly medicine makes known to me the seriousness of
my malady, on the other hand, it gives me grounds for
thinking that I am not incurable. Surely so wise a
Physician, nay, a Physician Who is Wisdom Itself,
would not apply in vain, would not waste a remedy of

infinite worth. But it is manifest that it would be
wasted not only if a cure could be easily obtained
without it, but also, and much more, if even with its
use a cure were impossible. Therefore, the hope I have
conceived animates me to the practice of penance and
powerfully inflames my desire to be cured. And I derive an increase of comfort from the angelic visitation
and allocution vouchsafed to the watching shepherds.
" Woe to you that are rich, for you have your consolation " from the things of earth, and are therefore unworthy of the consolations of heaven !   How many
noble, according to the flesh, how many mighty,
how many of the wise of this world were resting
on their soft beds at that hour, and not one of
them was deemed worthy to witness the new light,
or to hear the glad tidings of great joy, or to
listen to the angels as they sang in the air, " Glory
to God in the highest." From this we should learn
that they who " are not in the labour of men," as the
Psalmist says, do not deserve to be visited by angels.
We should learn also how pleasing to the inhabitants
of heaven is the labour of him whose intention is pure
and spiritual, since they honour with their speech, and
with speech so delightful, even such as toil for the
support of their bodies, and under the compulsion of
corporal necessity. For in this way they show their
respect for that law imposed on the human race by
God, when He said to Adam, " In the sweat of thy
face shalt thou eat bread."

I entreat you, dearest brethren, to consider more
attentively how much God has done for your instruc-
tion and salvation.   Otherwise His words may be
found unfruitful in you, His words so " living and

efficacious," so "faithful and worthy of all acceptation," and expressed more by the labour of action than by the breath of the mouth. Do you suppose, my brethren, that it would be only a small disappointment to me did I know that these words which I am now addressing to you were destined to die in your hearts without producing any fruit? And who am I or what are my words? If, then, a man of such little consequence, yea, of no consequence at all, grieves to behold the "labour of his lips," insignificant though it be, expended to no purpose, with how much greater reason shall the anger of the Lord of Majesty be enkindled against us, if by our negligence or hardness of heart, we bring to naught the mighty works He has accomplished for our salvation? May He Who, in order to save us, consented to assume the servile form, may He deign to guard His poor servants from so dreadful a misfortune, for He is the Only-Begotten of the Father and is over all things God blessed for ever. Amen.

FOURTH SERMON FOR CHRISTMAS DAY

ON THE VIRTUES COMMENDED TO US BY THE NATIVITY

" And this shall be a sign unto you : you shall find the Infant wrapped in swaddling clothes and laid in a manger."— Luke ii. 12.

How great is the solemnity of Christmas you may recognise, my dearest brethren, from the fact that the day is too short for its celebration, and the wide-extended earth too narrow. It must spread itself out in space and in time. It invades the realms of night and occupies both heaven and earth. For the " night was illuminated as the day " when in the midst of its course that new light from above shone round about the shepherds. And in order that we might know where this joyous festivity began to be celebrated, there suddenly appeared " a multitude of the heavenly army, praising God," and the shepherds were told that the " great joy " already experienced by the angels, " shall be (communicated) to all the people." This is the reason why the present feast is regarded as more solemn than any other, and is more joyously kept " in psalms and hymns and spiritual canticles " ; and in the offices of to-day especially, we may believe, without the slightest hesitation, that the celestial " princes go before joined with singers, in the midst of young damsels playing on timbrels."

How many altars are glittering to-day with gems and gold ! How many churches are decorated with costly hangings! But do you suppose that the angels of God will be attracted by this earthly splendour, and will turn away in disgust from the rags of the poor? If such be the case, how is it that they showed themselves of old, not to the kings of the earth, or to the priests of the temple, but rather to the " shepherds keeping the night-watches over their flock "? How is it that the Saviour Himself, to whom belong all the earth's treasures of silver and gold, has consecrated and sanctified poverty in His own Person? How is it, also, that the angel makes such deliberate reference to the poverty of the new-born Child? For not without a certain purpose and mysterious significance was the Saviour wrapped in swaddling clothes and laid in the manger, since this was expressly offered as a sign to the shepherds: " This shall be a sign unto unto you," said the Angel, " you shall find the Infant wrapped in swaddling clothes and laid in a manger." Thus, O Lord Jesus, even Thy poor swaddling clothes have been " set for a sign," and " for a sign which (is) contradicted " by many to this day. " For many are called, but few are chosen," and few, consequently, signed.* Brethren, I recognise now, I recognise " Jesus the (great) High-Priest" Who was " clothed with filthy garments" whilst He disputed with the devil—I am speaking to persons who know the Scriptures and are familiar with the symbolic vision vouchsafed the

---

* " And I saw another angel ascending from the rising of the sun, having the sign of the living God; and he cried with a loud voice to the four angels to whom it was given to hurt the earth and the sea, saying: hurt not the earth, nor the sea, nor the trees, till we sign the servants of our God in their foreheads. And I heard the number of them that were signed: an hundred and forty-four thousand were signed of every tribe of the children of Israel " (Apocalypse vii. 2-4).

Prophet Zachary.* But when our Divine Head had triumphed over the enemies of our salvation, He at once "clothed Himself with a change of garments," He "put on beauty," and appeared covered "with light as with a garment," giving us an example, that as He has done so we should do also. For although an iron breast-plate is not so light and graceful as a linen robe, it is more serviceable in time of war. But the day will come when the members shall follow their Head, and then the whole body shall sing with one voice and one spirit, "Thou hast turned for me my mourning into joy : Thou hast cut my sackcloth, and hast compassed me with gladness."

"You shall find the Infant wrapped in swaddling clothes and laid in a manger." Thus spoke the Angel. And a little further on we read of the shepherds how "they came with haste, and they found Mary and Joseph, and the Infant lying in the manger." Now, what is the meaning of this ? The Angel appears to have mentioned only the humble Infant, and yet the shepherds find not the Infant alone, but Mary and Joseph also. Perhaps the celestial herald had a particular desire to commend to us the virtue of humility, embodied in the new-born Babe, because he had himself stood firm in humility when his brother-angels fell

* "And the Lord shewed me Jesus the high-priest standing before the angel of the Lord : and Satan stood on his right hand to be his adversary. And the Lord said to Satan : The Lord rebuke thee, O Satan : and the Lord that chose Jerusalem rebuke thee : Is not this a brand plucked out of the fire ? And Jesus was clothed with filthy garments : and he stood before the face of the angel. Who answered and said to them that stood before him : Take away the filthy garments from him. And he said to him : Behold I have taken away thy iniquity, and have clothed thee with change of garments " (Zachary iii. 1-5).

through pride. Or perhaps the reason why he made special mention of what belongs to humility is this: in order to teach us that it is by humility more than by any other virtue we are to honour the Majesty of God. But humility is never found alone, since God always " giveth grace to the humble." Therefore the shepherds found " Mary and Joseph, and the Infant lying in the manger." For as the infancy of the Saviour manifestly designates the virtue of humility, in the same way is continence represented by the Virgin, and justice by Joseph, whom the Evangelist calls " a just man," and " whose praise is in the Gospel." Who does not know that purity is a perfection which belongs to one's own flesh ? Justice, on the contrary, has regard to one's neighbour, being the virtue which inclines us to give every man his due. And humility has relation to God, because it reconciles us to Him, makes us subject to His law, and renders us pleasing in His sight. Hence the holy Virgin said, " He hath regarded the humility of His handmaid." Consequently he who violates continence, sins against his own body ; he who violates justice, sins against his neighbour ; and he who by pride and self-exaltation violates humility, sins against God. The first degrades himself, the second oppresses his neighbour ; the third dishonours God, so far as it depends on him. The Lord says, " I will not give My glory to another." But the proud man replies, " Although Thou refusest to give me Thy glory, I will nevertheless take it." For pride is not pleased with the division made by the angels, when they sang, " Glory to God in the highest, and on earth peace to men of good will." The proud man, therefore, does not worship God, but is rather lifted up against Him with manifest impiety and infidelity. What indeed is piety but the worship of God? And how can anyone really worship God unless he voluntarily subjects himself to Him, so as to be able to say with the Psalmist, "As the eyes of the handmaiden are on the hands of her mistress, so are the eyes of my heart on the Lord, our God"?

Therefore, my brethren, let us "live soberly, and justly, and godlily in this world," if we desire to find always in ourselves "Mary and Joseph, and the Infant lying in the manger." For it was unto this that "the grace of God our Saviour hath appeared, instructing us"; and if we are faithful in the practice of these virtues, the glory of God also shall be revealed to us. We have the testimony of St. Paul for this. "The grace of God our Saviour," he says, "hath appeared to all men, instructing us that, denying ungodliness and worldly desires, we should live soberly, justly, and godlily in this world, looking for the blessed hope and coming of the glory of the great God and our Saviour Jesus Christ." Grace hath appeared in the Little One, but this Little One "shall be great," as the Angel Gabriel predicted of Him. And those whom the Little One shall have instructed unto humility and meekness of heart, shall hereafter be made great and glorious at the coming of the great and glorious God, Our Lord Jesus Christ, Who is over all things and blessed for evermore. Amen.

FIFTH SERMON FOR CHRISTMAS DAY

On Man's twofold Misery and the twofold Mercy of God, and on the Consolation which the poor find in the Nativity

" Blessed be the God and Father of our Lord Jesus Christ, the Father of mercies and the God of all comfort, Who comforteth us in all our tribulation."—1 Cor. i. 3-4.

Blessed be the Father " for His exceeding charity wherewith He loved us," and sent us His own Beloved Son, in Whom He is well-pleased, to reconcile us by His death that we might " have peace with God," and to become Himself not only the Mediator but also the Pledge of our reconciliation. With so loving a Mediator, my brethren, we have no need to be disquieted; and with so faithful a Pledge, there is no cause for diffidence. But you will say, " What manner of Mediator is He Who is born in a stable, is laid in a manger, is wrapped in swaddling clothes like other infants, weeps like other infants, and lies weak and helpless like other infants ? " Nevertheless, He is in truth a most powerful Mediator, and is seeking the things that are to our peace, not negligently (as we do ourselves), but zealously and efficaciously, even in this state of seeming impotence. He is indeed an Infant, but the infant Word of God, Whose very infancy is divinely eloquent. " Be comforted, be comforted, My people, saith your God." This is what Emmanuel, God with us, is saying to us now. This is what the stable is crying out to us, and the manger, and the Infant's tears, and the clothes that cover Him. The stable announces that a shelter is provided for the poor man who fell among robbers. The manger reminds us that food is being ministered to the same man who " is compared to senseless beasts and is become like them." The tears and swaddling clothes proclaim that his raw wounds are being washed and bound up. For Christ has no need of such things. He wants none of these for Himself, but all are for His chosen. " They will reverence My Son," said the Father of mercies. They will, indeed, O Lord, and they do reverence Him. But who ? Not the Jews to whom He was sent, but the elect for whose sake He was sent.

For we reverence Him in the manger, we reverence Him on the cross, we reverence Him in the sepulchre. Lovingly do we embrace our God, become a tender Child for us; lovingly do we honour Him, all covered with blood for our sakes, pale with the pallor of death for our sakes, laid in the tomb for our sakes. Most devoutly do we adore our Infant Saviour with the Magi; most affectionately do we clasp Him to our breast, with holy Simeon, " receiving Thy mercy, O God, in the midst of Thy Temple." For He is the Same of Whom we read, " The Mercy of God is from eternity." Surely there can be nothing co-eternal with the Father save the Son and the Holy Ghost. And Each of these Two is not so much merciful, as Mercy Itself. But the Father Himself is also Mercy. And these Three are not three mercies, but one Mercy, just as They are one Essence, one Wisdom, one Divinity, one Majesty. Nevertheless, since God is called the " Father of mercies," who does not see that the name of Mercy specially and by appropriation designates the Son ?

And justly is He called the "Father of mercies," "to Whom it is natural to show mercy always and to spare."

But some one may object to this, and say, "How is it natural to Him 'to show mercy always,' since His 'judgments are a great deep,' according to the Psalmist? Neither is it said that 'all His ways are mercy,' but that 'all His ways are mercy and truth,' that is, mercy and justice. And the same Prophet implies that He is not less just than merciful, in the words, 'Mercy and judgment I will sing to Thee, O Lord.'" I grant all this, my brethren. "He hath mercy on whom He will, and whom He will He hardeneth." Still I say it is natural for Him to show mercy, for He finds in His own Divine Nature the motive and impulse to this. But if He also judges and condemns, that is because we compel Him, as it were, to do so. And thus it is clear that mercy proceeds from His Heart in a manner very different from punishment. But listen to what He says Himself by the Prophet Ezechiel, "Is it My will that a sinner should die, saith the Lord God, and not that He should be converted from his ways and live?" Rightly, therefore, is He called, not the Father of judgments, or of vengeance, but the "Father of mercies"; not only because mercy appears to belong more to a father than indignation, and because "as a father hath compassion on his children, so hath the Lord compassion on them that fear Him"; but also and especially because (as I have said) He discovers in Himself alone the motive and impulse to show mercy, whereas when He exercises judgment or vengeance the cause is in us.

But it may be further asked, wherefore then is He

called the "Father of *mercies*," rather than the Father of *mercy* ? " God hath spoken once," says the Psalmist, " these two things have I heard, that power belongeth to God, and mercy to Thee, O Lord." But the Apostle represents to us this same mercy as manifold in the one Word, in the one Son, when he calls God " the Father," not of one mercy, but " of mercies," and " the God " not of some, but " of *all* comfort, Who comforteth us in *all* our tribulation." " The mercies of the Lord are many," as the Prophet Jeremias in his turn bears witness ; and they need to be many, since " many (also) are the afflictions of the just, and out of them all will the Lord deliver them." One is the Son of God, and the Word is but one ; whilst our manifold misery demands not only great mercy, but even " a multitude of tender mercies." Yet perhaps on account of the two substances which are united in man, namely, the flesh and the spirit, and in each of which he is miserable, we may speak not improperly of human misery as twofold ; although in reality man is subject to a multitude of miseries, both in body and in soul. Many in truth are the tribulations we suffer in our material and in our spiritual part, but He Who " made the whole man sound on the Sabbath day," delivers us from all our necessities. Since, therefore, the one and Only-Begotten Son of the Father has already come for the sake of our souls, viz., to " take away the sins of the world," and is to come again for the sake of our bodies, to raise them up and to make them " like to the Body of His glory," it ought not to seem unreasonable if I say that this twofold mercy is acknowledged when God is called the " Father of mercies." For by taking to Himself the two elements of our human

nature, the soul, namely, and the body, He, the Lord
our God, seems to say to us, " Be comforted, My people,"
not once only, but with reiteration, as before through
His Prophet, " Be comforted, be comforted, My people."
Thus are we given assurance that He, Who did not
disdain to assume both our flesh and our spirit, has
also the will to save both.

But whom do you think He will thus save ? His
own people, doubtless. For even now, at His first
coming, " He will save—not everyone, but—His people
from their sins." And, in like manner, it is not every
body, but only the " body of our lowness " that shall
hereafter be "made like to the Body of His glory."
It is therefore His own people He comforts, that is,
" the humble people " whom He will save, as the
Psalmist testifies, when He will " bring down the eyes
of the proud." Shall I tell you more clearly who are
His people ? " To Thee is the poor man left," says
the man according to God's own heart. And Christ
Himself says in the Gospel, " Woe to you that are
rich, for you have your consolation." Would that we,
my dearest brethren, were always desirous to be found
amongst that happy people, who, so far from being
threatened with woes, are rather comforted by the
Lord their God ! Why, indeed, should He comfort
those who have their own consolation ? No, the speechless Babe in the manger offers no consolation to the
garruolus ; the tears of the Infant Christ do not comfort
the lovers of mirth ; His poor swaddling clothes suggest
nothing consoling to them that " wish to walk in long
robes " ; the crib and the stable have no comforting
lesson for such as " love the first seats in the syna-
gogues." But perhaps they will declare themselves

satisfied to let all this consolation go to those who " wait with silence for the salvation of God," to those who mourn, and to those who are clad in the livery of the poor. Let them know, therefore, that the angels also will comfort none others. For it is to the " shepherds watching and keeping the night-watches over their flock " that the joy of the new light is announced, and for them the Saviour is said to be born. Upon the poor and the toiling—not upon you that are rich and " have your consolation," and with it the divinely-denounced woe—the " day of sanctification has dawned " amid the watches of the night, so that the " night (is) illuminated as the day," or is rather changed into day, since the Angel says, not " this night," but " this day is born to you a Saviour." For "the night is passed and the Day is at hand," the true Day of true Day, the Salvation of God, our Lord Jesus Christ, Who is over all things and is Himself true God, blessed for evermore. Amen.

ST. BERNARD'S HYMN TO THE NAME OF JESUS

"Jubilus Rhythmicus Sancti Bernardi"

I

The very thought of Jesus thrills
  With transports sweet this heart of mine,
But oh ! what joy, what rapture fills
  The soul that sees His Face divine !

II

No sweeter sound can soothe the ear,
  The voice no sweeter song can sing,
No sweeter thought the soul can cheer,
  Than Jesus, Son of heaven's King.

III

Jesus, the sinner's hope of grace,
  To all who ask how loving kind !
How good to all who seek Thy Face !
  But what, oh, what to them that find !

IV

O Jesus, sweetness of my heart,
  The Fount of life, and light, and love,
To me the joy of joys Thou art,
  A joy all hope and thought above.

V

Nor tongue nor pen can ever tell,
How eloquent soe'er they be,
'Tis only he that loves Thee well
Can know the joy of loving Thee.

VI

I'll seek Him where He loves to hide,
Within the cloister of my breast,
I'll seek at home, I'll seek outside,
I'll seek with love that cannot rest.

VII

With Mary, at the dawn of day,
I'll seek the tomb where Jesus lies,
In spirit, not with eyes of clay,
Lamenting with love's plaintive cries.

VIII

My tears upon the stone shall beat,
My sobs and groans shall fill the place,
I'll cast me down at Jesus' Feet
And clasp them close in fond embrace.

IX

How good a King our Jesus is !
How great a Conqueror of hell !
All beautiful whate'er is His
And sweet beyond my power to tell.

X

Stay with us still, Lord Jesus, stay,
　To guide our steps life's desert through ;
Drive from our souls all mists away,
　And let Thy love the world subdue.

XI

The sun of truth shines bright and clear
　Within the soul where Thou art guest ;
How vile the things of earth appear
　When Thy sweet love inflames the breast !

XII

The love of Jesus brings delight
　And ravishment exceeding great,
Its tenderness no man aright,
　Though thousand-tongued, can celebrate.

XIII

His Passion is a proof of this,
　His streaming Wounds attest the same,
Whereby He bought us heaven's bliss
　And saved us from the vengeful flame.

XIV

Acknowledge Jesus, mortals all,
　The grace to love Him boldly claim,
With fervour seek Him, great and small,
　And let the search your hearts inflame.

XV

Yea, love Him Who so loveth you,
    Let love's debt liquidated be,
Give love for love and so pursue
    The odour of His charity.

XVI

O Jesus, Source of clemency,
    Our only joy and hope Thou art ;
All grace and sweetness flows from Thee,
    The true delight of every heart.

XVII

Jesus, my Treasure, let me feel
    The fullest force of love divine,
Oh, let me in Thy presence kneel
    And see the glory that is Thine !

XVIII

I cannot speak in worthy wise
    Of Thee, yet shall not silent be ;
The will and daring love supplies,
    For all my soul is set on Thee.

XIX

Thy love, O Lord, is mystic meat,
    Which brings no weariness to the mind ;
It fills us with refreshment sweet,
    Yet leaves the hunger still behind.

XX

For he that eats Thee hungers still,
  Who drinks Thee feels intenser thirst,
One only good attracts his will :
  With him 'tis Jesus last and first.

XXI

How Jesus savours none can tell
  But he whom love possesses whole ;
How blest who Jesus loves so well
  That all things else disgust his soul !

XXII

O Jesus, name to angels dear,
  As honey in the mouth Thou art,
As sweetest music in the ear,
  As heavenly nectar in the heart.

XXIII

I'm weary waiting, Jesus mine,
  Thy coming ; when, when shall it be ?
When shall Thy Face upon me shine ?
  When shall my soul be filled with Thee ?

XXIV

Thy love which ever in me lives,
  With languor constant grieves the mind,
But joyous is the pledge it gives
  Of life, by limits none confined.

XXV

O Jesus, boundlessly benign !
  O Goodness inexpressible !
Let love my heart unite with Thine
  Who canst alone its hunger still.

XXVI

How good to love and seek Thee, yea,
  And for Thy sake all else disown !
To die to self, that so I may,
  Sweet Jesus, live for Thee alone !

XXVII

O Jesus, sweetness over all,
  The love-sick's soul one remedy,
These tears of love upon Thee call,
  My inmost heart cries out for Thee.

XXVIII

For Thee I pine in every place,
  And languish for Thy presence sweet.
What bliss whene'er I see Thy Face !
  What joy when I may clasp Thy Feet !

XXIX

Then such caresses, such delights
  As make all other savours sour !
For Jesus then Himself unites
  To me for one too short-lived hour.

XXX

What long I've sought I now can see,
 I've reached the goal of my desire ;
I languish, Lord, with love of Thee,
 And all my soul seems set on fire.

XXXI

When love divine to this attains,
 No passion can oppose its sway,
It never dies, it never wanes,
 But stronger grows from day to day.

XXXII

Thy love, O Jesus, ne'er can lose
 Its heat, but burns for ever bright ;
Its savour, wondrous sweet, imbues
 And fills the soul with pure delight.

XXXIII

This love, descending from the pole,
 Abides in me, a welcome guest,
It sets on fire my very soul,
 And makes a heaven in my breast.

XXXIV

O happy flame of charity !
 O blissful ardour of desire !
O love of God's sweet Son ! In thee
 Is shelter safe from passion's fire.

XXXV

O Virgin's Offspring, Jesus mine !
My sole delight and dearest love !
To Thee be praise and power divine,
Be Thine the kingdom bright above !

XXXVI

Come, come, Lord Jesus, best of kings,
A brighter radiance on me cast ;
Come, Source whence light eternal springs,
So long desired, come, come at last.

XXXVII

Thy brightness, Jesus, shames the sun,
No fragrance can with Thine compete,
Thy loveliness the palm hath won,
Than sweetness' self Thou art more sweet.

XXXVIII

Thy savour, Lord, gives such delight,
Thy perfume is so sweet withal,
My love-sick soul longs for the sight
Of Thee, Who art her all in all.

XXXIX

For Thou love's consummation art,
The bliss and sunshine of my mind,
The pride and glory of my heart,
O Jesus, Saviour of mankind.

XL

Reseat Thee at the Father's Right,
    Beloved Lord, Thy work is done ;
Thy foes Thou hast subdued with might,
    And now enjoy the kingdom won.

XLI

Yet we can never parted be,
    For Thou hast stolen away my heart :
Go where Thou wilt, I'll follow Thee,
    Sweet Lord, who all my glory art.

XLII

Lift up your gates and run to meet,
    Ye angels all, your King and mine ;
And thus the glorious Victor greet :
    " Hail Jesus, hail our King divine."

XLIII

Great King of glory, Lord of might,
    Immortal Conqueror of hell,
Sole Splendour of the land of light,
    And Giver of all grace as well ;

XLIV

Yea, mercy's never-failing source,
    Eternal Brightness of the blest :
Drive clouds and sadness from our course
    And let Thy light upon us rest.

XLV

The angels with unwearying voice
  Shall sing Thy praises evermore,
For that Thou didst the world rejoice
  And peace 'twixt God and man restore.

XLVI

The Prince of peace is Jesus mine,
  Of peace no mind can comprehend;
For this my soul shall ever pine,
  To this do all her strivings tend.

XLVII

Our Jesus has the skies resought,
  To rule as King o'er friends and foes,
And my poor heart has with Him brought,
  Which follows Him where'er He goes.

XLVIII

Oh, let us honour Him with prayer,
  With praise, and vows, and hymns of love,
That through His mercy we may share
  His glory in the realms above.